WOW! Smart Reading

1

Mihee Kim
Mihee Kim graduated from Ewha Womans University and has been teaching English at an elementary school for more than ten years. She has written a number of books for children and adults, including *10 Hours English Grammar, Catch-Up with Good English Writers' Secrets, Yo! Yo! Play Time Level 1,* and *EBS English After-School.* She leads E·NEXT, an association of English education experts.

Joel Landry
Joel Landry graduated from Saint Mary's University, in Halifax, Canada and has worked with elementary students for more than ten years. He has been teaching English in Korea for the past six years and currently teaches at Yong In University.

Yoonjung Lee
Yoonjung Lee has been teaching children for more than ten years. She wrote several columns and books at Design-Kids. She created a science program for children and directed many other programs.

Publisher	Kyudo Chung
Editorial Director	Juyon Choi
Editors	Kyunghee Jang, Seunghyeon Oh
Proofreader	Michael A. Putlack
Art Director	Hyeonseok Jeong
Designers	Taeho Ha, Kyuok Jeong
Photo Credit	www.shutterstock.com

First published in January 2012 by
DARAKWON, Inc.

Darakwon Bldg., 211, Munbal-ro, Paju-si, Gyeonggi-do, Republic of Korea
Tel: (02) 736-2031 (Ext. 250)
Fax: (02)732-2037

Price ₩13,000
ISBN 978-89-277-0340-2
      978-89-277-0349-5 (set)

www.darakwon.co.kr

Reviewers
Soomin Kim (Jungtap Elementary School)
Sejin Han (Sujin Elementary School)

Contributors
Bona Jin (Chungsol Elementary School)
Seonok Lee (OK's Class)
Jongsam Jeon (JS New York English Academy)
Kyounghi Park (Kwangnam Elementary School)
Sunguk Han (Bundang High School)

Illustrated by Doyun Kim

[Components] • Student Book • Workbook • 1 Audio CD
            8 7 6 5 4 3 19 20 21 22 23 24

To Teachers and Parents

WOW! Smart Reading is a noteworthy course to systematically develop students' reading skills in English. This course is specially designed to improve students' comprehension ability by having them read informative and creative passages. Students can learn essential reading and thinking skills step by step while reading the combined nonfiction and fiction passages in one topic. **WOW! Smart Reading** is unique because it integrates nonfiction and fiction passages in each unit. **WOW! Smart Reading** is a three-level course containing 8 units in each level. Each unit revolves around interesting topics by integrating creative fiction stories and informative nonfiction passages. Included in each unit are sections to assess reading comprehension and to organize information using graphic organizers and summaries. The questions in this course are the types used on various English tests and school exams. The unique model on which this course is designed provides readers with a fresh approach to learn English. As students work through **WOW! Smart Reading**, they may forget they are studying. What a great way to learn English!

Special Features:

Warm Up & Get Ready
Students are asked some open-ended questions using pictures for motivation to preview the unit. Key vocabulary is presented with simple activities in which students match words with corresponding pictures and choose or write words in a sentence.

Reading Passages with Reading Skills
Students read interesting nonfiction and fiction passages. The Reading Skills section in each lesson helps students learn the main idea and basic reading skills in the reading passage.

Comprehension Check Up
After reading the passages, students answer reading comprehension questions such as checking true or false, choosing the correct answers, or filling in the blanks.

Grammar Connection
This section provides students with grammar practice by using the major grammar points in the reading text of each lesson.

On Your Own
Students review the key structure or main idea from each lesson by using sequencing, graphic organizers, Venn diagrams, or summaries.

Wrap Up
Students can test themselves on what they learned in the unit through two short nonfiction and fiction passages and with questions. The question types are based on various English tests and school exams.

We hope students improve their reading ability with this series.

Mihee Kim, Joel Landry, Yoonjung Lee

Contents

Book 2	Book 3
Unit 1 Flat Stanley	**Unit 1** Eating the Rainbow
Unit 2 A Special Festival	**Unit 2** Summer Camp
Unit 3 Pirates of the Caribbean	**Unit 3** The Cinco de Mayo Festival
Unit 4 Tasty Food	**Unit 4** Healthy Living
Unit 5 Nanobots	**Unit 5** A Work of Nature
Unit 6 The Native American Tipi	**Unit 6** The Human Skeleton
Unit 7 Be Creative	**Unit 7** American Football
Unit 8 Discovering Other Planets	**Unit 8** The Green Earth

Unit	Theme	Topics	Reading Skills	Grammar
1 UNIT	Super Senses	**(Nonfiction)** animals' super senses **(Fiction)** a superhero with super senses	• Main Idea • Main Idea and Details • Searching for Information	• does, doesn't • of + noun/gerund
2 UNIT	Reptiles	**(Nonfiction)** an alligator and a Komodo dragon **(Fiction)** flying with a baby dragon	• Main Idea • Compare and Contrast • Story Elements	• have, has • under, out, behind, around
3 UNIT	Appearances	**(Nonfiction)** how to describe what people look like **(Fiction)** twins change their hairstyles	• Main Idea • Description • Compare and Contrast	• noun • -s (simple present tense)
4 UNIT	Plants	**(Nonfiction)** helpful plants **(Fiction)** a girl who loves the jungle	• Main Idea • Problem and Solution • Main Character	• help + verb • verb + -ed (past tense)

Unit	Theme	Topics	Reading Skills	Grammar
5 UNIT	Unique Food	• **(Nonfiction)** unique food in the world • **(Fiction)** food made with insects	• Main Idea • Searching for Information • Sequence	• plural nouns • positions of adjectives
6 UNIT	Amazing Story	• **(Nonfiction)** dolphins rescued from danger • **(Fiction)** a dolphin show	• Main Idea • Problem and Solution • Sequence	• subject and predicate • simple subject and predicate
7 UNIT	Hand Gestures	• **(Nonfiction)** various hand gestures • **(Fiction)** the origin of the phrase "thumbs up"	• Main Idea • Describing • Details	• Wh questions • be + verb-ing
8 UNIT	Balls	• **(Nonfiction)** features of balls • **(Fiction)** a soccer game	• Main Idea • Details • Problem and Solution	• when • can, cannot

How to Use This Book

Welcome to **WOW! Smart Reading**.

This three-level series will help students improve their reading skills.
Each unit has two lessons related to the same topic. Lesson 1 is nonfiction. This lesson gives students in-depth knowledge on the topic. Lesson 2 is fiction. The second lesson allows students to explore the topic in a fun way that stimulates their creative thinking.

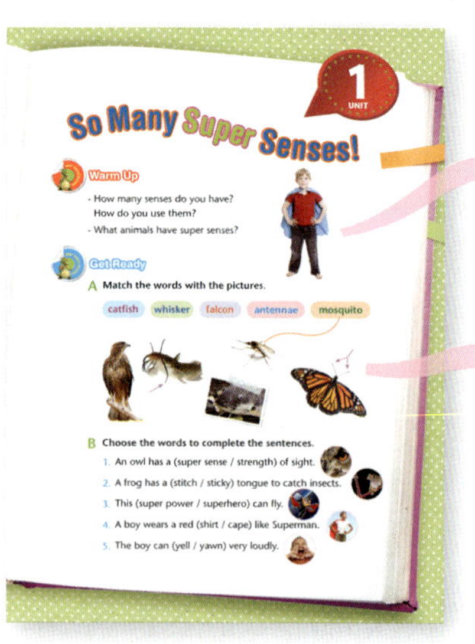

Warm Up

Students answer questions using the picture to preview the unit and think about what they will read.

Get Ready

Students learn the key words which they will read in the passage.

Lesson 1, 2

Students read two passages based on the topic of the unit.
Lesson 1 is nonfiction.
Lesson 2 is fiction.

Reading Skills

Students understand the passage in greater detail by learning various essential reading skills.

Comprehension Check Up

Students comprehend the passage by answering questions about the passages that they have read.

Grammar Connection

Students work through key grammar points found in the passage. They learn the grammar from the sentences in the passage in a natural way.

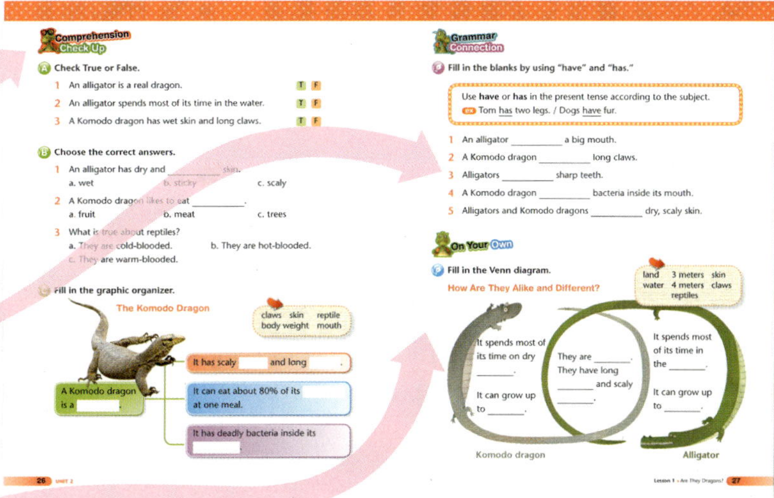

On Your Own

Students review the main idea of the passage by completing the graphic organizer, Venn diagram or summary.

Wrap Up

Students read short passages related to lessons 1 and 2 and then answer the questions to wrap up.

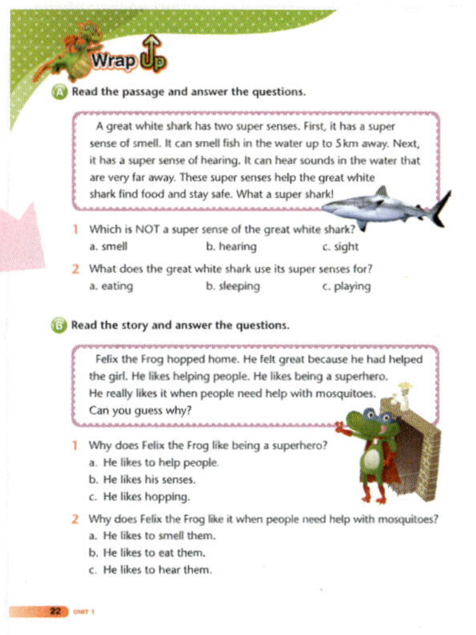

Workbook

•Vocabulary Review
Students review the vocabulary including the key words in the unit. Then, students practice them by completing the sentences.

•Dictation
Students listen to the passages in the student book again and fill in the blanks.

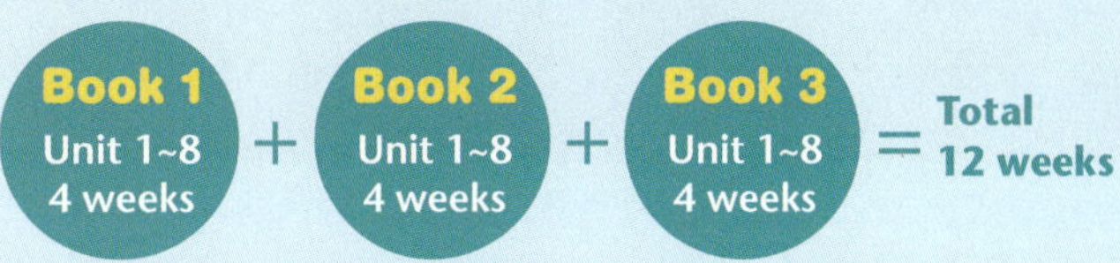

Lesson Schedule

Each unit will take 2 hours to complete.
If you study for 4 hours (2 times) a week,
you can finish one book in 4 weeks.

Book 1 Unit 1~8 4 weeks + **Book 2** Unit 1~8 4 weeks + **Book 3** Unit 1~8 4 weeks = **Total 12 weeks**

Reading Skills in This Book

Main Idea and Details

A main idea is the most important topic. It tells what all or most of the sentences are about. The main idea helps readers understand the most important information in the passage. Details are statements that support the main idea by describing, explaining, or giving information about it.

Fact and Opinion

A fact is true information. An opinion is defined as a personal feeling, thought, or belief.

Cause and Effect

A cause is an event that shows why something happens. An effect is something that happens as a result of a cause. One cause can have several different effects.

Story Elements

The elements of a story include the setting, characters, and plot. The setting describes where and when the story takes place. The characters are the people, places, or things that take part in the story. The plot describes the pattern of events that take place in the story.

Searching for Information

To search means to look for something. In a story, readers must often look for specific information to improve their understanding.

Problem and Solution

A solution is a way to fix the problem. A problem is something that causes trouble. The plot of a story usually begins with a problem and ends with a solution.

Compare and Contrast

When considering two or more ideas or objects, to compare them is to note their similarities. To contrast them is to note their differences. This skill shows how things are alike or different.

Sequence

The sequence is the order in which events happen in the story. To identify the order, look for time signal words.

Description

To describe is to explain in detail the characteristics or properties of a person, place, object, idea, etc.

Describing Pictures

Describing pictures involves looking at a picture and finding an explanation of what you see. It can include explaining a picture's meaning, main idea, and details.

LET'S GO!
WOW! Smart Reading 1

So Many Super Senses!

Warm Up

- How many senses do you have?
  How do you use them?
- What animals have super senses?

Get Ready

A Match the words with the pictures.

catfish whisker falcon antennae mosquito

B Choose the words to complete the sentences.

1. An owl has a (super sense / strength) of sight.

2. A frog has a (stitch / sticky) tongue to catch insects. 

3. This (super power / superhero) can fly.

4. A boy wears a red (shirt / cape) like Superman. 

5. The boy can (yell / yawn) very loudly. 

ANIMALS WITH SUPER SENSES

Some animals have super senses. Their senses are much better than ours.

You taste with your tongue. Can you taste with your whole body?

5 A catfish tastes with its whole body. It can even taste with its whiskers. A catfish has a super sense of taste.

You see with your eyes.

10 How far can you see? You can see a small mouse from 10 meters. A falcon can see the same mouse from 1,500 meters. A falcon has a super sense of sight.

15 You smell with your nose. You can smell meat cooking on a barbecue from 10 meters. A wolf can smell meat from 1,000 meters. A wolf has a super sense of smell.

A butterfly has many super senses.

A butterfly has compound eyes. It can see in all directions without turning its head. A butterfly has a super sense of sight.

5 A butterfly doesn't have a nose. Then how does it smell? It smells with its antennae. A butterfly has a super sense of smell.

A butterfly doesn't have a tongue. Then how does it taste? It tastes with its feet.

10 A butterfly's sense of taste is one of its super senses. A butterfly doesn't have ears. Then how does it hear? It feels sound with the hairs on its wings. It has a super sense of hearing.

Wow! What amazing creatures! Unlike us, 15 they have many super senses.

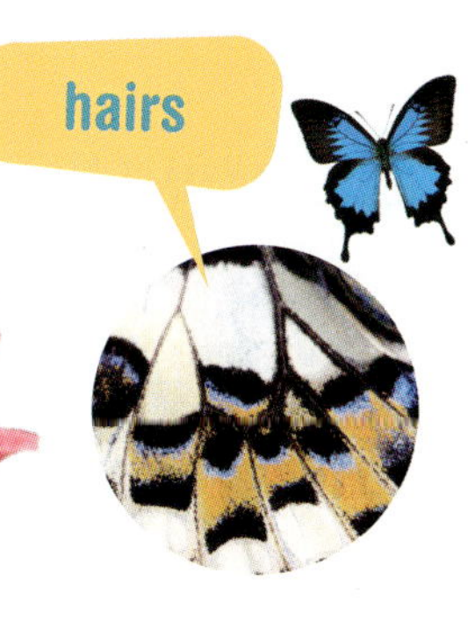

- **Main Idea**
This story is mainly about (super senses / super strength).
- **Main Idea and Details**
Circle the sentence that shows the main idea.
Underline the sentences that show the details.

Comprehension Check Up

A **Check True or False.**

1 A wolf has a super sense of taste. T F

2 All animals have super senses. T F

3 A falcon has a super sense of sight. T F

B **Choose the correct answers.**

1 A catfish uses its ___________ to taste.
a. tongue   b. whole body   c. nose

2 A butterfly has ___________ super senses.
a. three   b. four   c. five

3 How does a butterfly taste?
a. with its tongue   b. with its wings   c. with its feet

C **Fill in the blanks with the words from the box.**

sees   hears
smells   tastes

1 A catfish ___________ with its body.

2  A butterfly ___________ with the hairs on its wings.

3 A wolf ___________ with its nose. 

4  A falcon ___________ with its eyes.

Grammar Connection

Fill in the blanks by using "does" and "doesn't."

> Make the sentences into questions or negative statements using **do(es)** or **do(es)n't**.
>
> **ex** Dolphins live in the sea. → <u>Do</u> dolphins live in the sea?
>
> A butterfly has ears. → A butterfly <u>doesn't</u> have ears.

1 A butterfly __________ have a nose.

2 How __________ a wolf smell?

3 Butterflies __________ have tongues.

4 How __________ owls see?

5 __________ a butterfly have a nose?

Fill in the graphic organizer.

Animals' Super Senses

catfish   wolf   butterfly
sight   super senses

Detail 1
A ________ has a super sense of taste.

Detail 2
A falcon has a super sense of ________.

Main Idea
Animals have __________.

Detail 3
A ________ has a super sense of smell.

Detail 4
A ________ has many super senses.

A SUPERHERO

Hi. I'm Felix the Frog. I am a **superhero**. I wear a blue mask and a red **cape**.

I have three super senses. I have a super sense of sight. I have big eyes that can see all around me. They are on the top of my head, so
5   I don't need to turn my head to look around! I have a super sense of hearing. I can hear high sounds through my ears and low sounds through my skin. I have a super sense of smell. I can find things by smelling.

I can also jump very high and have a **sticky** tongue to catch things.
10 These are not super senses, but they help me as a superhero.

Late one night, someone **yelled**, "Help me!"

The sound was coming from an old house. Inside the house was a girl.

"Help me, please!" she cried. "There are **mosquitoes** in my house.

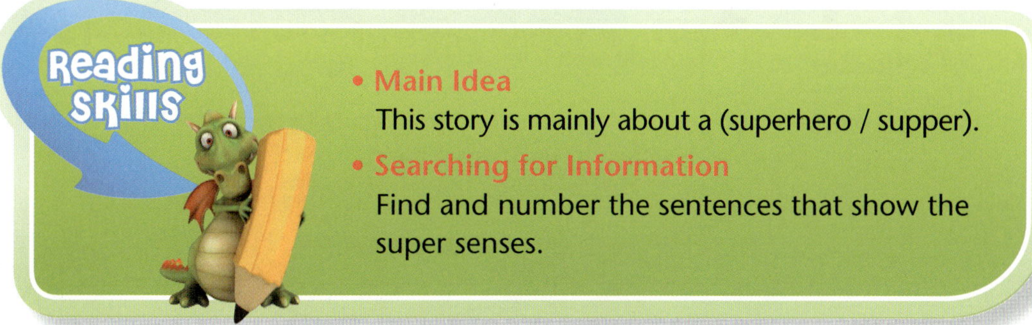

They are too small, and I cannot see them. They are biting me."

"Mosquitoes? No problem! I can find them," I said.

With my super sense of sight, I looked around. She was right. There were many mosquitoes. I smelled the mosquitoes with my super sense of smell. Then, I jumped around as high as I could. Using my sticky tongue, I began to eat the mosquitoes. Soon, all the mosquitoes were gone.

"Oh, thank you. You helped me. By the way, who are you?" asked the girl.

"I am Felix. I like to help people," I said.

"Wow, you are a real superhero," she said.

Comprehension Check Up

A) Check True or False.

1 Felix the Frog can see all around himself. T F

2 Felix the Frog has a yellow cape. T F

3 Felix the Frog has a sticky tongue. T F

B) Choose the correct answers.

1 Felix the Frog has ___________ super senses.
  a. three   b. four   c. five

2 The ___________ were biting the girl.
  a. frogs   b. dogs   c. mosquitoes

3 How did Felix the Frog help the girl?
  a. He ate the mosquitoes.
  b. He jumped around the house.
  c. He smelled the mosquitoes.

C) Fill in the graphic organizer.

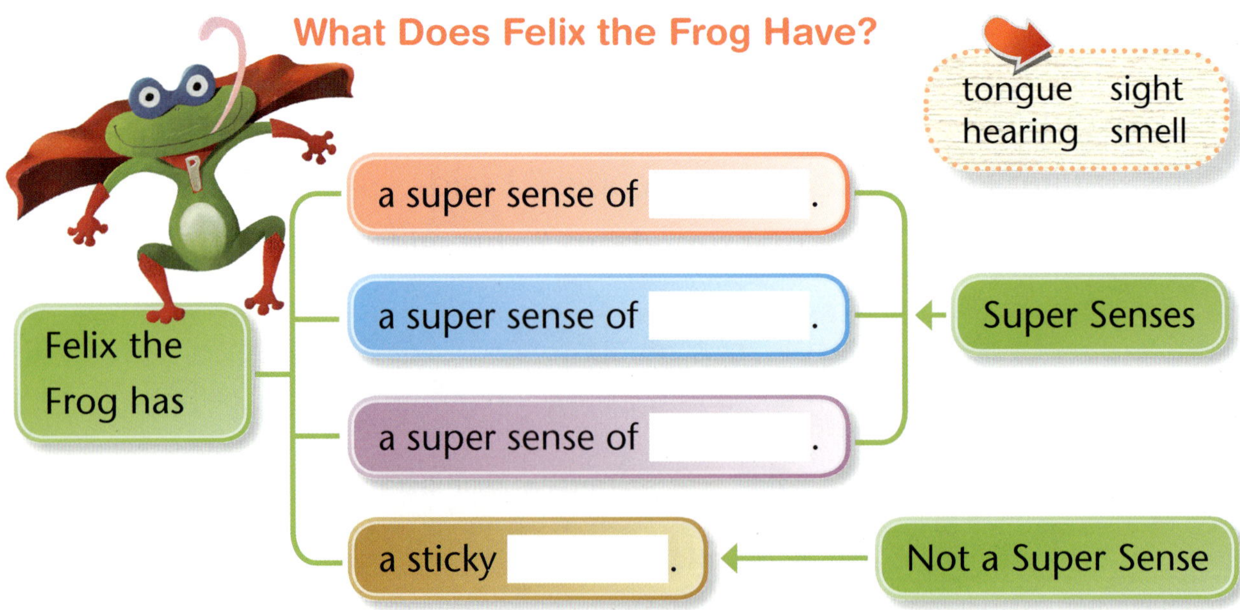

Grammar Connection

Fill in the blanks by using "of + noun/gerund."

> Use a noun or gerund (verb + -ing) after the preposition **of**.
> **ex** I have a sense <u>of taste</u>.
> I have a super sense <u>of hearing</u>.

1   Felix the Frog uses his nose for his super sense ___________________.

2   He uses his ears for his super sense ___________________.

3   People use their tongue for their sense ___________________.

4   Felix the Frog uses his eyes for his super sense ___________________.

5   Felix the Frog's big eyes are on the top ___________________.

Complete the sentences in the correct order.

How Does Felix the Frog Save the Day?

1   Felix ___________________________.

2   Felix ___________________________.

3   Felix ___________________________.

4   Felix ___________________________.

- jumps around the room
- eats the mosquitoes
- hears someone yelling
- sees the mosquitoes

Wrap Up

A **Read the passage and answer the questions.**

> A great white shark has two super senses. First, it has a super sense of smell. It can smell fish in the water up to 5 km away. Next, it has a super sense of hearing. It can hear sounds in the water that are very far away. These super senses help the great white shark find food and stay safe. What a super shark!

1 Which is NOT a super sense of the great white shark?

   a. smell   b. hearing   c. sight

2 What does the great white shark use its super senses for?

   a. eating   b. sleeping   c. playing

B **Read the story and answer the questions.**

> Felix the Frog hopped home. He felt great because he had helped the girl. He likes helping people. He likes being a superhero. He really likes it when people need help with mosquitoes. Can you guess why?

1 Why does Felix the Frog like being a superhero?

   a. He likes to help people.

   b. He likes his senses.

   c. He likes hopping.

2 Why does Felix the Frog like it when people need help with mosquitoes?

   a. He likes to smell them.

   b. He likes to eat them.

   c. He likes to hear them.

What Does It Look Like?

Warm Up

- What kind of animal does it look like?
- Whose eye is it?

Get Ready

A Draw lines to match the words for this animal.

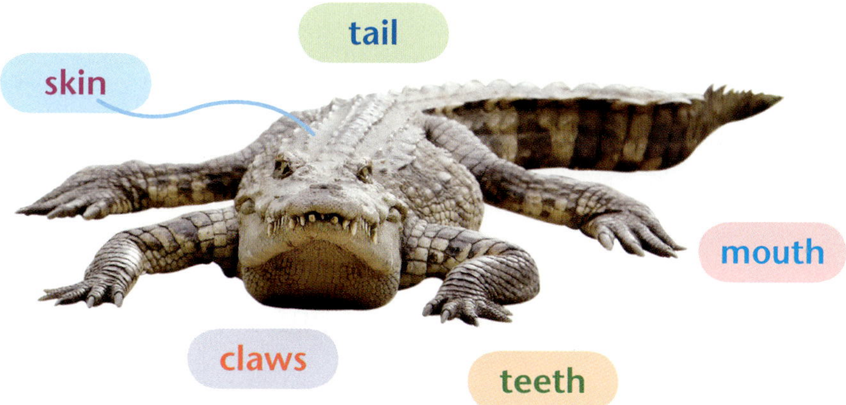

B Choose the words to complete the sentences.

1. A (dragon / dolphin) is a legendary animal that looks like a reptile.

2. This animal (weighs / waits) 15 kilograms.

3. It has (skate / scaly) skin.

4. Snakes and crocodiles are (reptiles / rats).

5. This dog can (bite / beg) people.

Are They Dragons?

Look at these animals. Are they **dragons** or not? Let's take a closer look at them.

This animal has a big **mouth** and sharp **teeth**. It likes to eat meat. This animal has dry, **scaly skin** and long **claws**. When it hunts, it doesn't use its claws. It opens its mouth wide to eat large **prey**. It spends most of its time in the water. Can you see its eyes on the top of its head? When it hides in the water, it can still see and catch its prey. It can grow up to 4 meters long and **weigh** up to 453 kilograms.

Look at this animal. It spends most of its time on dry land. It is
very big, but it can run very fast. It can grow up to 3 meters long and
weigh up to 70 kilograms. This animal has dry, scaly skin. It likes to eat
meat. It uses its long claws to hunt prey. When it eats, it can eat up to
80 percent of its body weight. It has deadly bacteria inside its mouth.
This means that when it **bites** animals, they can become sick and die.

These animals look like dragons, but they are not real dragons.
They are **reptiles**. Reptiles lay eggs and are cold-blooded. This means
that they need the sun to stay warm. One is an alligator. The other is a
Komodo dragon. Can you guess which ones they are?

Comprehension Check Up

A **Check True or False.**

1 An alligator is a real dragon. T F

2 An alligator spends most of its time in the water. T F

3 A Komodo dragon has wet skin and long claws. T F

B **Choose the correct answers.**

1 An alligator has dry and ___________ skin.
a. wet b. sticky c. scaly

2 A Komodo dragon likes to eat __________.
a. fruit b. meat c. trees

3 What is true about reptiles?
a. They are cold-blooded. b. They are hot-blooded.
c. They are warm-blooded.

C **Fill in the graphic organizer.**

The Komodo Dragon

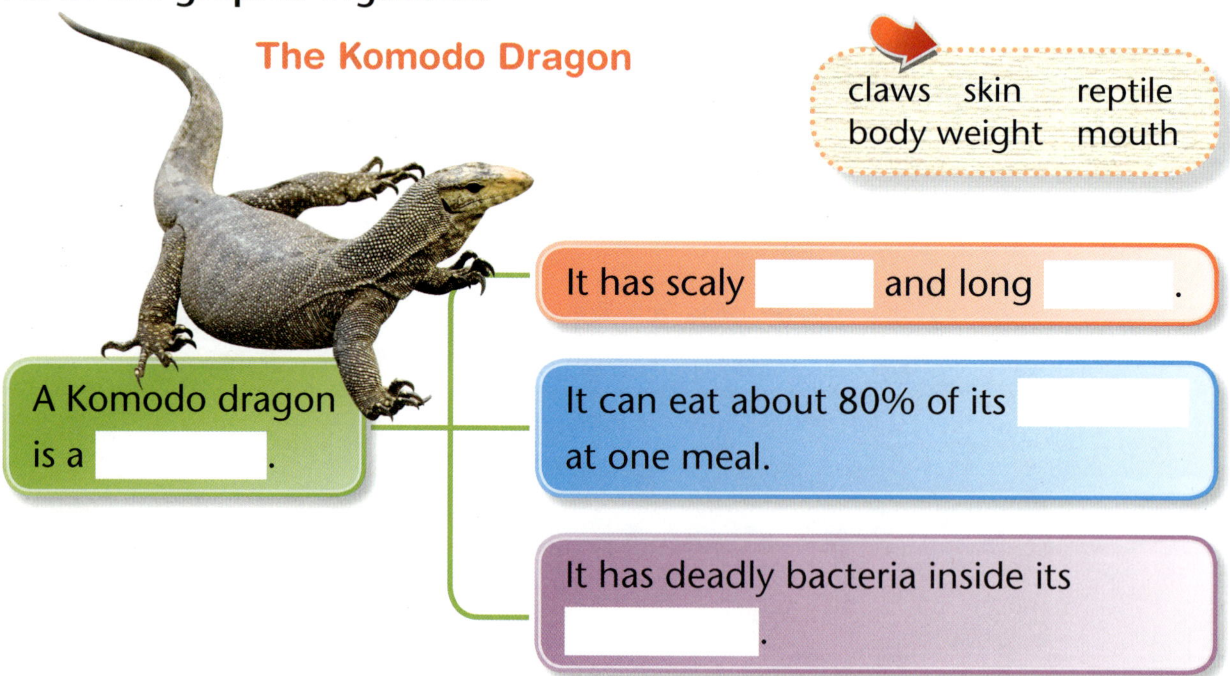

Grammar Connection

Fill in the blanks by using "have" and "has."

Use **have** or **has** in the present tense according to the subject.
ex Tom <u>has</u> two legs. / Dogs <u>have</u> fur.

1 An alligator ____________ a big mouth.

2 A Komodo dragon ____________ long claws.

3 Alligators ____________ sharp teeth.

4 A Komodo dragon ____________ bacteria inside its mouth.

5 Alligators and Komodo dragons ____________ dry, scaly skin.

On Your Own

Fill in the Venn diagram.

How Are They Alike and Different?

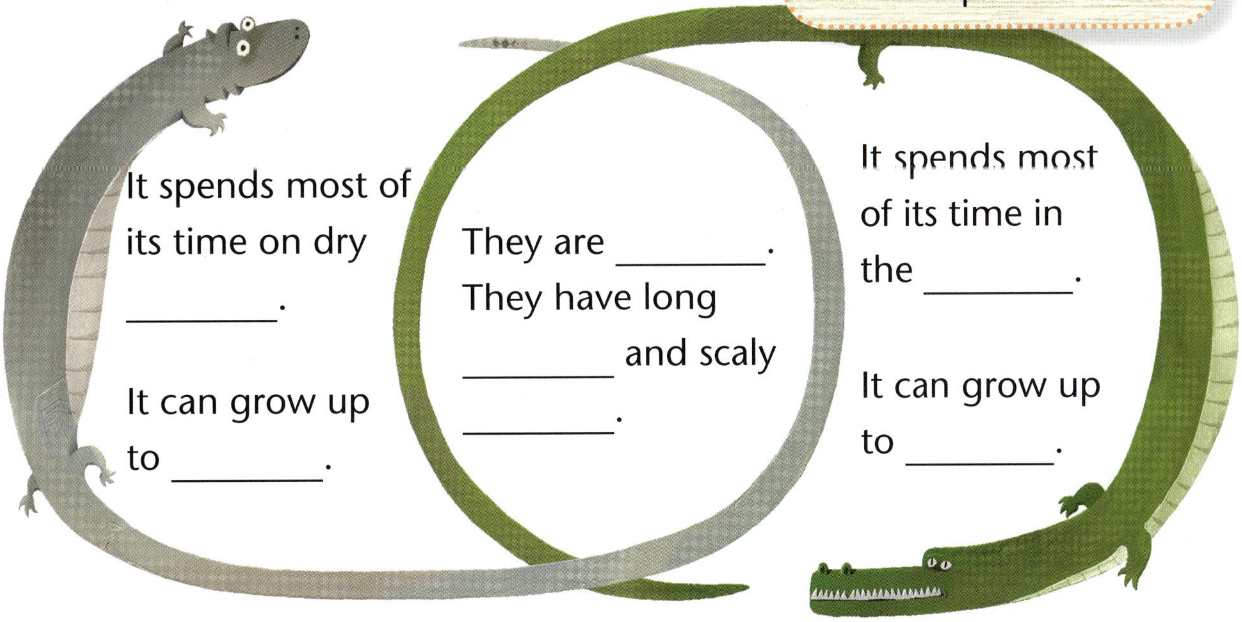

Komodo Dragon

Alligator

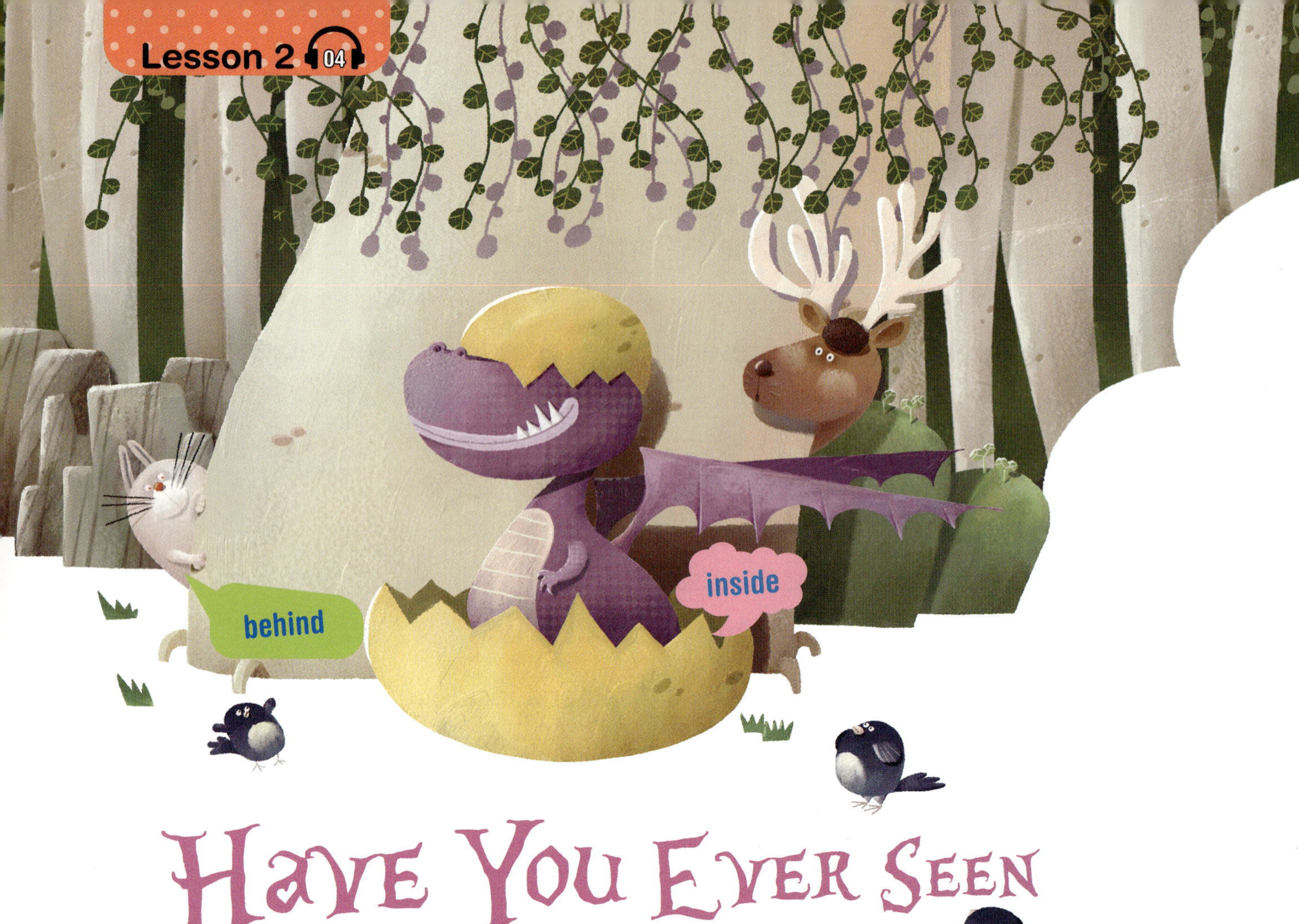

Have You Ever Seen a Dragon Fly?

Deep in a green forest, an egg is under a tree. The egg is big and yellow. What kind of egg is it?

Shh! Something is moving inside the egg. It wants to come out. The egg begins to crack. Something is using its claws to come out of the egg. Small claws push through the crack, and the egg opens. Aha! It is a dragon egg.

A baby dragon comes out of the egg. The baby dragon is purple. It has claws and scaly skin. It has a long, hard tail. It looks like a reptile but is different. The baby dragon has two big wings.

At that same time, a boy named Daniel is walking in the green forest. He hears a strange sound. He sees something around the corner of a rock.

"Hmm… What is that? It looks like a tail," says Daniel.

Just then, a baby dragon comes out from behind the rock.

"Oh my! You're a dragon. You're so cute. What's your name?" asks Daniel.

The baby dragon does not say anything. It just looks at Daniel.

"Umm. Dio! I'll name you Dio. Dio, can you fly?" says Daniel.

Dio says, "Sure! I can fly with my wings. Come and ride on me. Where do you want me to fly?"

Daniel gets on the dragon and says, "Fly wherever you want. But don't hit any trees!"

The dragon flies over the trees, above the forest, and up to the clouds. Daniel has a big smile.

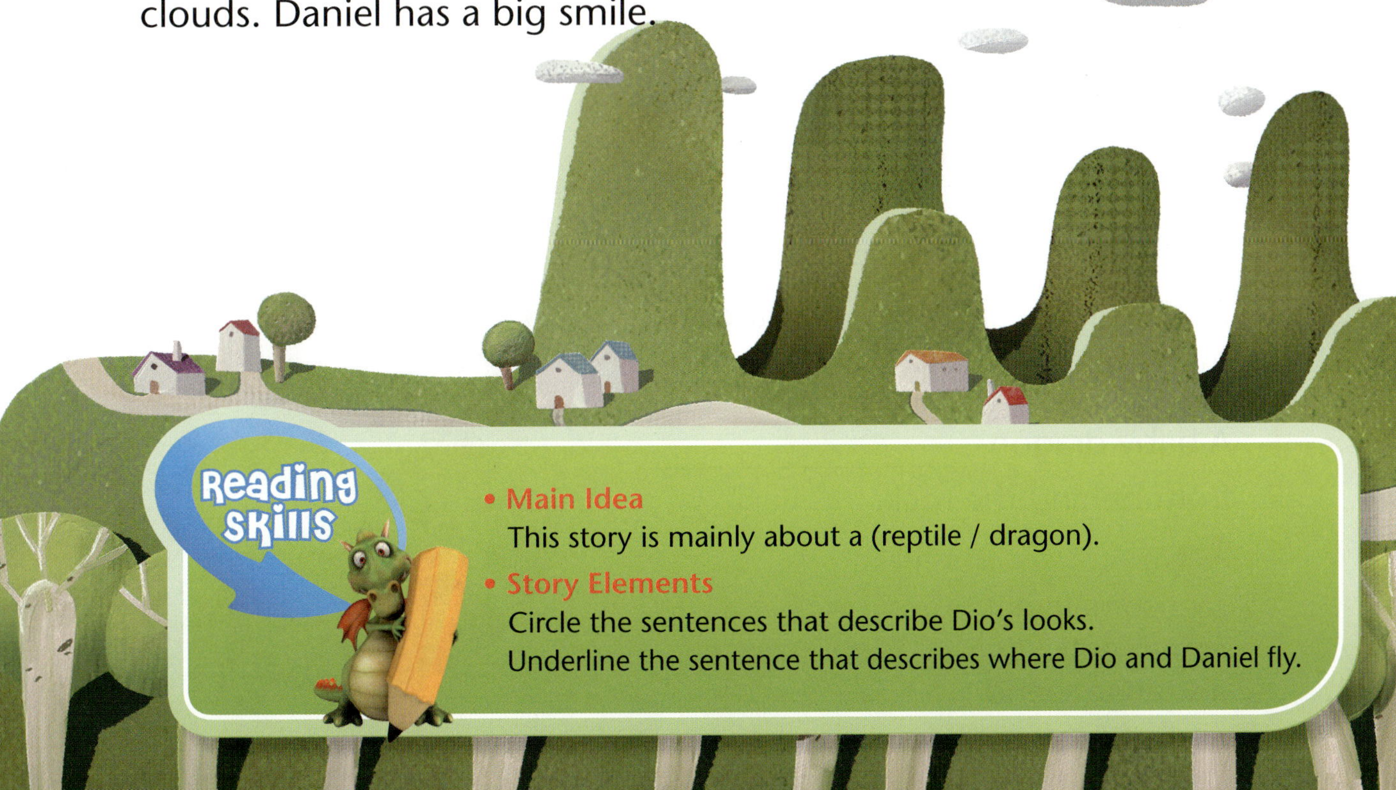

- **Main Idea**
This story is mainly about a (reptile / dragon).
- **Story Elements**
Circle the sentences that describe Dio's looks.
Underline the sentence that describes where Dio and Daniel fly.

Comprehension Check Up

A **Check True or False.**

1 The dragon egg is small and green. T F

2 The baby dragon uses its claws to crack the egg. T F

3 The baby dragon is a reptile. T F

B **Choose the correct answers.**

1 This story is about a ____________.
   a. baby dragon   b. baby reptile   c. green forest

2 Something is moving ____________ an egg.
   a. under   b. around   c. inside

3 What will happen at the end of the story?
   a. The dragon won't fly away.
   b. Daniel and the dragon will become friends.
   c. Daniel and the dragon will have a fight.

C **Fill in the blanks with the phrases from the box.**

How Does Daniel Meet the Dragon?

1 Daniel hears ____________________.

2 Daniel ____________________ around the corner of a rock.

3 A baby dragon ____________________ from behind the rock.

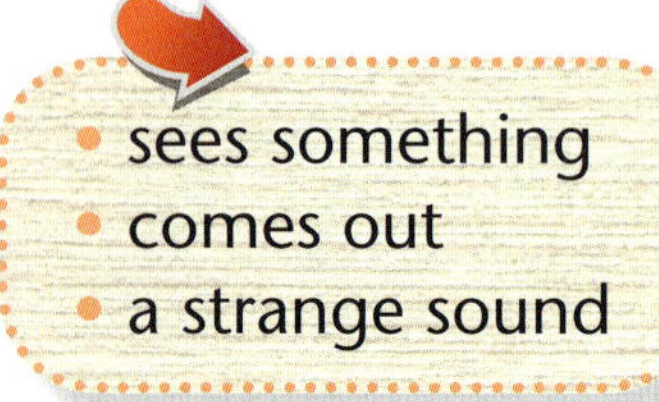

Grammar Connection

Fill in the blanks by using the prepositions in the box.

Use prepositions of place such as **under**, **out**, **behind**, and **around**.

1 A egg is ____________ the tree.

2 A baby dragon comes ____________ of the egg.

3 Something is moving ____________ a rock.

4 The dragon is ____________ the rock.

On Your Own

Write the sentences in the correct order.

The Story of Daniel and the Dragon

1 Daniel finds something behind the rock.

2 ____________________ Can you fly?

3 Sure! ____________________

4 ____________________

- Ride on me.
- Are you a dragon?
- Fly high to any place.

Wrap Up

A **Read the passage and answer the questions.**

> There are many kinds of reptiles all over the world. Alligators, snakes, lizards, and turtles are reptiles. Reptiles have dry skin with scales on their bodies. They are cold-blooded. So they warm themselves by lying in the sun.

1 Which animals are NOT cold-blooded?

a. lizards   b. alligators   c. birds

2 Which animal group stays warm by lying in the sun?

a. insects   b. reptiles   c. birds

B **Read the story and answer the questions.**

> Daniel and Dio are flying high. The wind is blowing Daniel's hair. They see a blue sky, white clouds, and green treetops. Far below, they see a Komodo dragon. The Komodo dragon looks at them with a jealous face. That's because the Komodo dragon can't fly, so it is jealous of them.

1 Why does the Komodo dragon feel jealous?

a. It wants to fly.

b. It wants to be a dragon.

c. It wants to eat Daniel and Dio.

2 Which is NOT true?

a. Daniel and Dio see a Komodo dragon.

b. The Komodo dragon can't fly.

c. The Komodo dragon doesn't want to fly.

Different Looks

Warm Up

- How do they look the same?
- How do they look different?

Get Ready

A Match the words with the pictures.

pigtail   bald   muscle   mustache   buzz cut

B Choose the words to complete the sentences.

1. I like her (dimples / dust) when she smiles.

2. I caught a cold, so I have a runny nose and a (straight / scratchy) throat.

3. She likes to (die / dye) her hair blue.

4. The (hairstylist / shopkeeper) cuts hair very well.

5. My friend (screams / sweeps) when he watches scary movies.

HOW DO THEY LOOK?

People have different looks. Look at the people around you. How do they look? Let's take a closer look at some other people.

Look at Mark. He has light skin. His eyes are big and blue. His hair is short and blond. He has a wide forehead and thin lips. He really likes to paint, so he is messy.

Look at Jenny. She is Mark's close friend. Her skin is neither dark nor light. Her eyes are brown and small. Jenny's hair is long and straight. And she has pigtails. She has dimples when she smiles.

Look at John. He is the principal of Mark's school. He is a short man with a **bald** head. He has a thin **mustache** that looks **scratchy**. He has wrinkles on his forehead and always
5 looks at students over his glasses.

Look at Michael. He is Mark's Physical Education teacher. He has a buzz cut. He is strong and has a lot of **muscles** on his body. His shoulders are very big. He
10 is neither tall nor short. He also has a charming smile.

People all around you can look different, but they can look nice. Think of some people you know. What do they look like? What about you? What do you look like? When you look in the mirror, ask yourself: How do I look?

Reading Skills

- **Main Idea**
  This story is mainly about different (looks / accessories).
- **Description**
  Circle the sentences that describe Mark's looks.
  Underline the sentences that describe Michael's looks.

A **Check True or False.**

1 Jenny doesn't have dimples when she smiles. T F

2 John is not bald but wears glasses. T F

3 Michael has a lot of muscles on his body. T F

B **Choose the correct answers.**

1 People have different ___________.
   a. dimples   b. looks   c. length

2 Mark's principal has something scratchy on his face. What is it?
   a. a whisker   b. a beard   c. a mustache

3 What is Michael's hairstyle called?
   a. pigtail   b. buzz cut   c. perm

C **Fill in the blanks with the words from the box.**

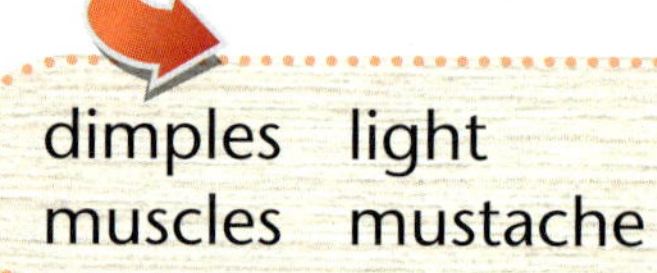

Different Looks

1 He has ___________ skin and big eyes.

2 He has ___________ when he smiles.

3 He has a thick ___________.

4 He has a lot of ___________ on his body.

Grammar Connection

Underline the "nouns" in each sentence.

> A **noun** is a word that names a person, place, or thing.
>
> **ex** His <u>name</u> is <u>Dave</u>.
>
> He is playing <u>soccer</u> on the <u>playground</u>.

1 Her eyes are very small.

2 His hair is short and blond.

3 He is the principal of a school.

4 He has wrinkles on his forehead.

5 He is strong and has a lot of muscles on his body.

On Your Own

Fill in the blanks with the words from the box.

What Do They Look Like?

> buzz cut   forehead
> straight   bald

He has a wide __________ and thin lips.

Jenny's hair is long and __________.

He has a __________ head and wears glasses.

He has a __________ and a strong body.

WHO IS WHO?

Reg and Shirley are siblings. They are twins, so they look alike. They both have light skin and big blue eyes. They both have shiny brown hair. And they both have bright white smiles. Even their voices are similar, so people cannot tell who is who.

5 Today, Reg and Shirley are going to a hair salon. They want new hairstyles. Reg thinks short hair looks good, so he wants a buzz cut. Also, he wants to dye his hair red. Red is his favorite color. Shirley thinks curly hair looks good, so she wants a perm. She wants her hair to be curly, just like her favorite singer. Reg and Shirley are excited 10 about their new hairstyles.

At the hair salon, Reg and Shirley meet Joan, the hairstylist. Reg tells Joan he wants short red hair. Shirley tells Joan she wants curly hair.

"No problem," says Joan. "Come and sit down."

Joan covers Reg and Shirley in large gowns to keep them clean. 15 Sitting in the chairs, Reg and Shirley feel sleepy. Soon, they are sound asleep.

Joan begins to cut their hair. Buzz, buzz, buzz. Snip, snip, snip. She styles the twins' hair. After a while, she is finished.

20 "Okay. I'm done. Open your eyes, kids," says Joan.

"Ahhhhhhhh!" screams Shirley.

"Noooooooo!" screams Reg.

"What's wrong?" asks Joan. "Don't you like your hairstyles?"

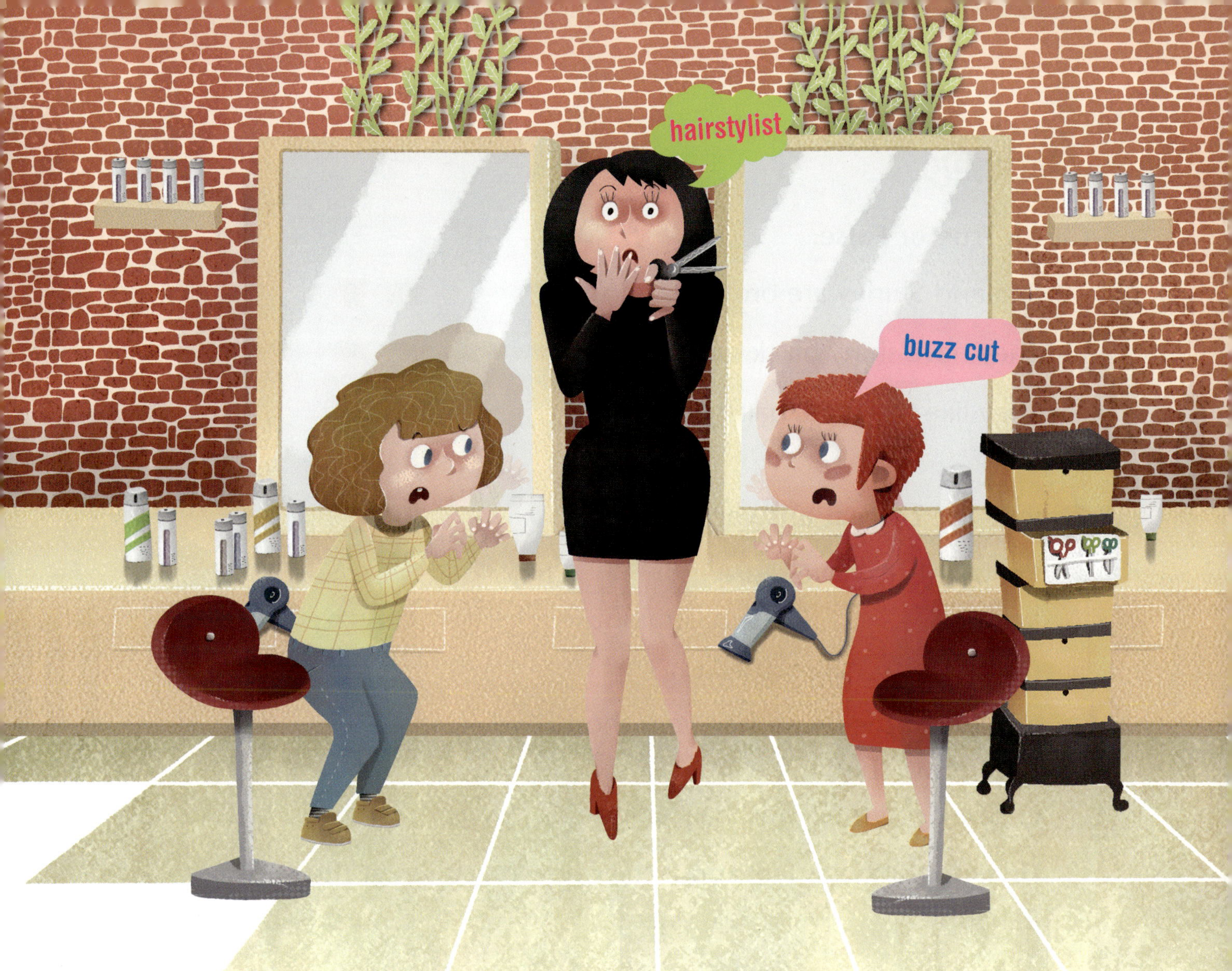

As Joan takes the gowns off Reg and Shirley, she sees the problem.
She made a mistake. She switched their hairstyles. Joan looks at Reg.
He has a beautiful curly perm. Joan looks at Shirley. She has a beautiful
red buzz cut.

5   "Oh, no!" says Joan.

• **Main Idea**
This story is mainly about (friends / twins) who change their
hairstyles.

• **Compare and Contrast**
Circle the sentences about the hairstyle Reg wants.
Underline the sentences about the hairstyle Shirley wants.

A **Check True or False.**

1 Reg and Shirley are brother and sister. T F

2 They have shiny black hair. T F

3 They like the same hairstyles. T F

B **Choose the correct answers.**

1 Reg wants to have red __________ hair.
   a. curly　　　　　　b. straight　　　　　　c. buzzed

2 What mistake did Joan make?
   a. She cut the twins' hair very short.
   b. She switched the twins' hairstyles.
   c. She dyed the twins' hair orange.

3 How do the twins feel about their new hairstyles at the end?
   a. happy　　　　　　b. sleepy　　　　　　c. surprised

C **Fill in the blanks with the words from the box.**

What Happened to Reg and Shirley?

large gowns
hair salon
twins
mistake

1 Reg and Shirley are __________. 

 2 Reg and Shirley go to a __________.

3 Joan covers Reg and Shirley in __________. 

 4 Joan made a __________. 

Grammar Connection

Write the correct forms by using the verbs given.

> Add **-s** at the end of a simple present tense verb in the third person singular.
> **ex** My mom <u>loves</u> me a lot.
> She <u>cooks</u> my favorite food for me.

1. She ___________ curly hair. (want)
2. Joan ___________ at Reg and Shirley. (look)
3. He ___________ red hair looks nice. (think)
4. She ___________ off the gowns. (take)
5. Joan ___________ the problem. (see)

Fill in the graphic organizer.

What Hairstyles Do They Want?

Wrap Up

A **Read the passage and answer the questions.**

Jake liked to eat lots of food. His favorite food was fried chicken and hamburgers. Jake was overweight. That made him sad. He wanted to be thinner. He exercised every day and changed his diet. Now, he looks different. He is slim and has more muscles. Do you want to change your looks, too?

1 Why was Jake sad?
a. He had muscles.
b. He was overweight.
c. He changed his diet.

2 How did Jake change his looks?
a. He ate meat.
b. He wore nice clothes.
c. He exercised and dieted.

B **Read the story and answer the questions.**

On the way home, Reg and Shirley look more closely at their new hairstyles. "I like red hair," says Shirley. "It looks nice with my red dress." "Yes, it does. And I like my curly hair," says Reg. "There is just one more problem," says Shirley. "We have to show Mom our new hair." "Oh, no!" say Reg and Shirley.

1 Do Reg and Shirley like their new hairstyles?
a. Yes, they do.
b. No, they don't.
c. No one knows.

2 Shirley says that her new hairstyle looks nice with her __________.
a. eyes
b. red dress
c. red shoes

Helpful Plants

 Warm Up

- What plants can you name?
- How do plants help you?

 Get Ready

A **Match the words with the pictures.**

cotton   hike   fever   medicine   walking stick

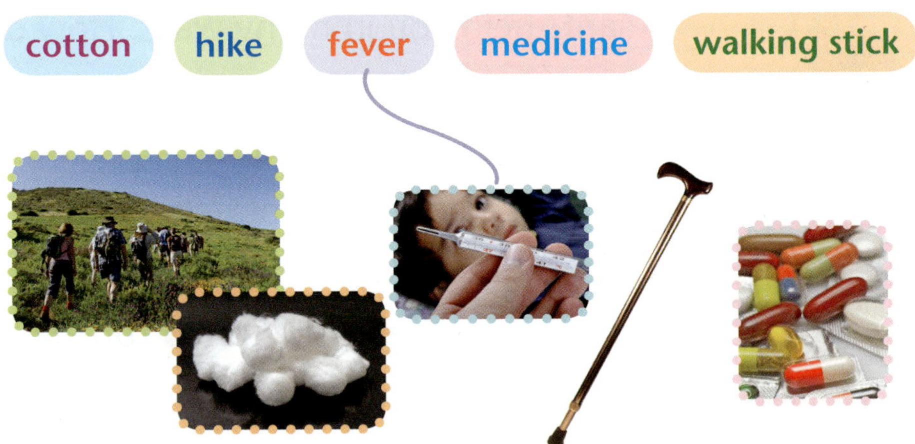

B **Choose the words to complete the sentences.**

1. It is hard to breathe when I have a (stuffed / long) nose. 

2. They went camping and made a (firefly / campfire).

3. The boy had a (stomachache / headache) after eating too much food.

4. Some plants can be very (helpful / highlighted).

5. The boy got (heart / hurt) when he fell down. 

HOW Do Plants Help You?

Plants help you in many ways. How do plants help you?

You eat food every day. Plants give you food to eat. Watermelon, potatoes, and carrots come 5 from plants. You wear clothes. Look at your clothes. Are they made of cotton? Some clothes are made of cotton. Cotton comes from a plant. Paper, tissue, and toys are made of wood. Wood comes from trees.

10 Some plants are used as medicine. When you are sick, some plants can make you feel better. If you have a stuffed nose, try some mint. It 15 helps clear your nose.

Aloe vera is a very helpful plant. It is green and juicy. People make helpful things with aloe vera. If you hurt your skin, put some aloe gel on it. It helps heal your skin. If your skin is dry, put some aloe cream on it.

5 Your skin will not feel dry. If you are dirty, wash with aloe soap. Aloe soap helps clean your skin.

Ginger is another helpful plant. Ginger is a root. If you have a stomachache, drink some ginger in tea or juice. It helps settle your stomach. If you have a fever, eat or drink

10 some ginger. It helps cool your fever. Ginger can also be used in food or candy.

Plants are helpful in your life. They give you food, clothes, medicine, and many other things.

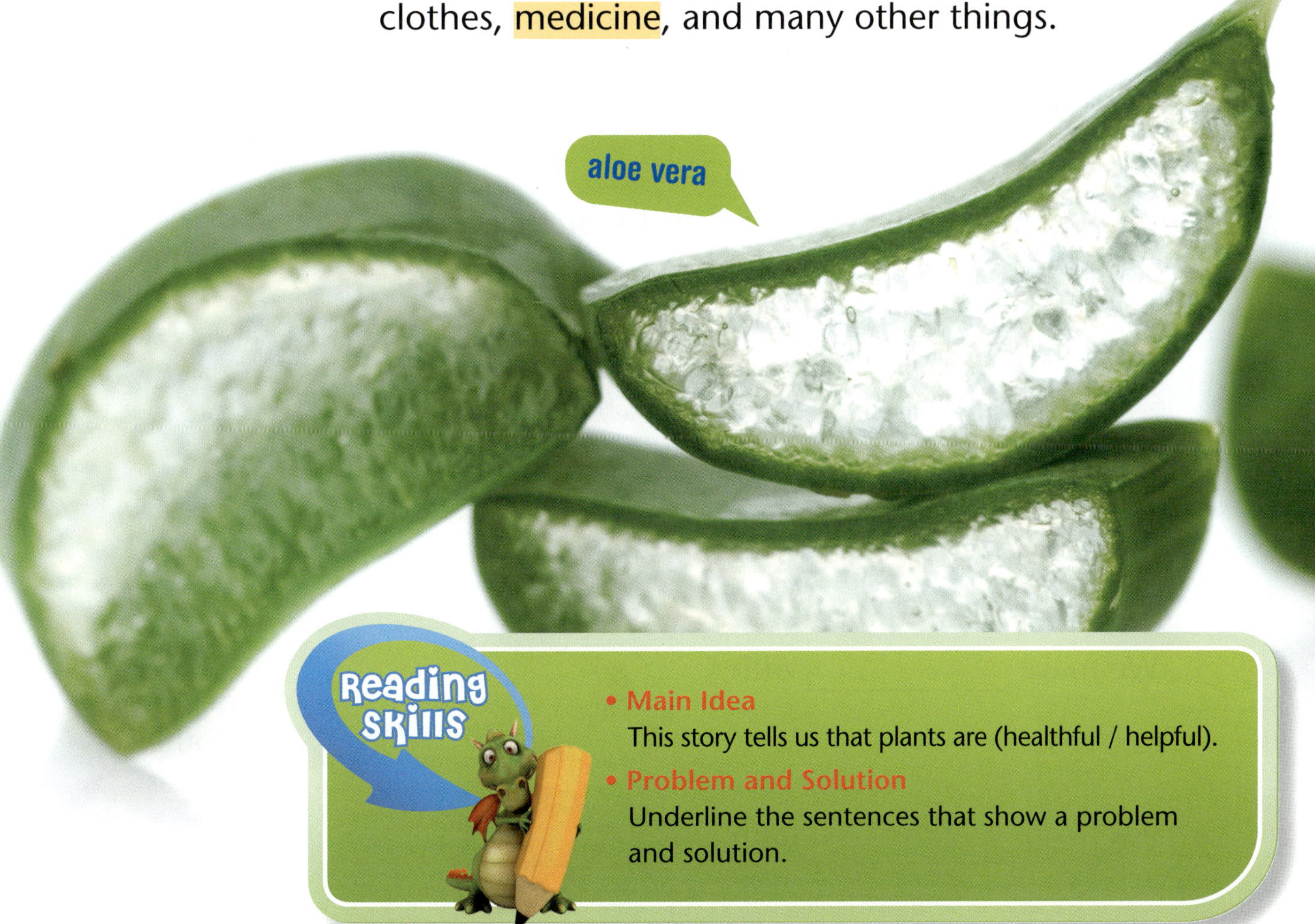

A Check True or False.

1 Some plants are used for food.　　　　　T　F

2 We use cotton for paper.　　　　　T　F

3 All plants are used as medicines.　　　　　T　F

B Choose the correct answers.

1 ____________ give you clothes, medicine, and many other things.
　a. Papers　　　　　b. Tissues　　　　　c. Plants

2 When you have a fever, ____________ will help cool your fever.
　a. ginger　　　　　b. watermelon　　　　　c. aloe vera

3 How are aloe vera and ginger similar?
　a. They are wet.　　　b. They help people.　　c. They are roots.

C Complete the sentences by using the pictures.

1 We make ____________ with  .

2 We make ____________ with  .

3 We make ____________ with  .

4 We make ____________ with .

gel
clothes
tissues
tea

Grammar Connection

Underline the verb after "help."

> Use the phrase **help + verb(bare infinitive)** in the sentences.
>
> **ex** I will <u>help feed</u> your dog. / She <u>helps wash</u> the dishes.

1 Ginger helps cool you down.

2 Mint helps clear your nose.

3 Aloe soap helps clean your skin.

4 Ginger helps settle your stomach.

5 Aloe gel helps heal your skin.

On Your Own

Fill in the graphic organizer.

How Do Plants Help You?

A Girl Named Jungle Jen

Please meet the girl, Jungle Jen. Do you know why her name is Jungle Jen? She likes to hike in the jungle.

One day, Jungle Jen was hiking in the jungle. She saw a big rock. Jen climbed the big rock. But she fell down. She hurt her hand. She needed some medicine to put on her hand.

Jen looked for an aloe vera plant. When she found one, she put aloe gel on her hand. Soon, her hand did not hurt anymore. Jen was happy because the plant healed her wound.

It was lunchtime. Jungle Jen felt hungry, so she found a mango tree. Jen loves to eat mangoes. Soon, she was not hungry anymore.

After eating, Jungle Jen walked in the jungle all day long. She felt tired. She looked for a stick. Jen found a good walking stick. She didn't feel tired anymore.

That evening, Jungle Jen began to get cold. She wanted to make a campfire. She looked for some wood. When she found some, Jen made a campfire. She was warm and felt sleepy next to the campfire. She wanted to sleep. She looked for some big leaves. When she found some, she made a soft bed.

That night, Jungle Jen slept very well. She was happy to have many helpful plants in the jungle.

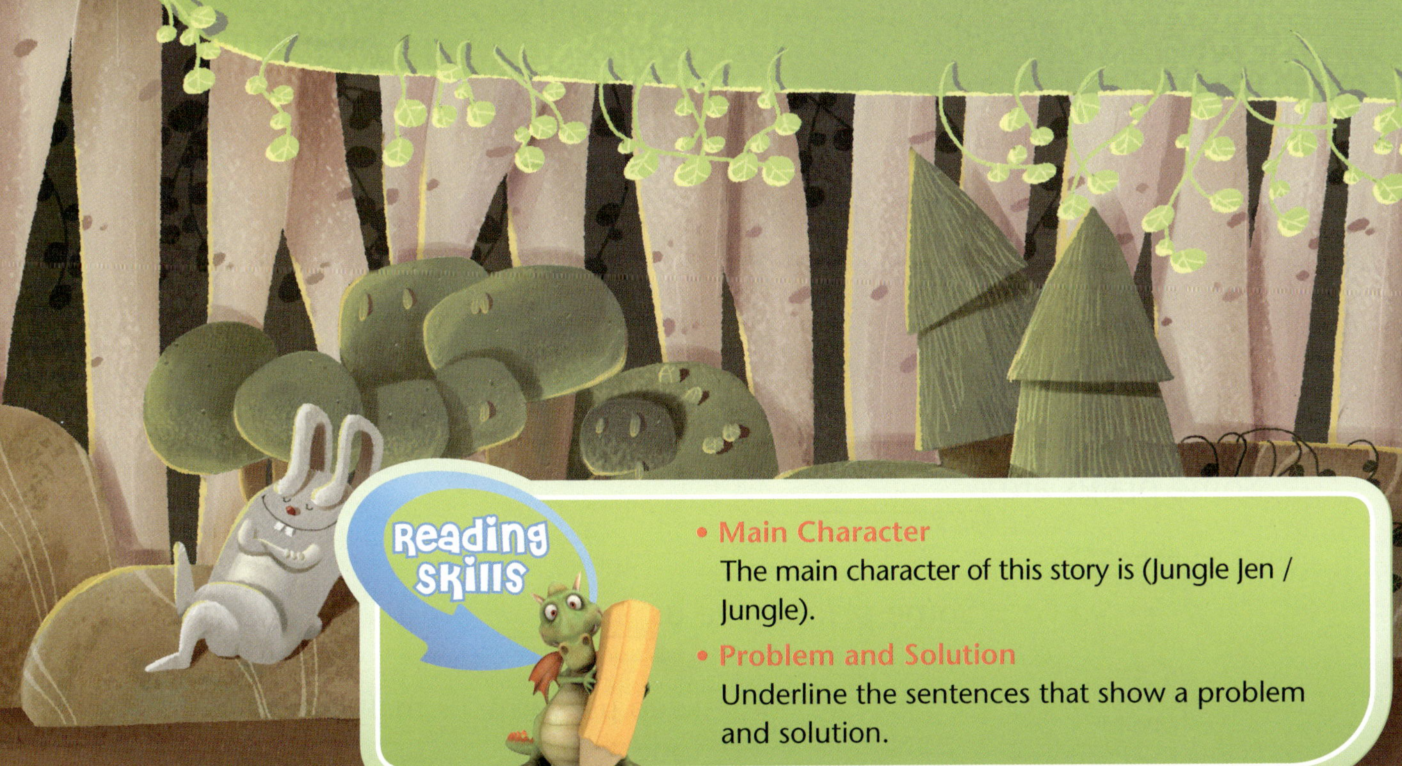

Comprehension Check Up

A **Check True or False.**

1 Jungle Jen doesn't like to go hiking.　　T　F

2 Jungle Jen climbed a tall tree.　　T　F

3 Jungle Jen put aloe gel on her hand.　　T　F

B **Choose the correct answers.**

1 Jungle Jen needed medicine because she ___________ her hand.
   a. burned　　　　　b. healed　　　　　c. hurt

2 Jungle Jen used ___________ to make a bed.
   a. sticks　　　　　b. wood　　　　　c. leaves

3 Why was Jungle Jen happy in the jungle?
   a. She liked to feel sleepy.　　　b. She made a campfire.
   c. There were many helpful plants.

C **Fill in the blanks with the phrases from the box.**

How Are Plants Helpful?

1 Some leaves can ___________ to sleep on.

2  Some wood can ___________.

3 Some plants are ___________.

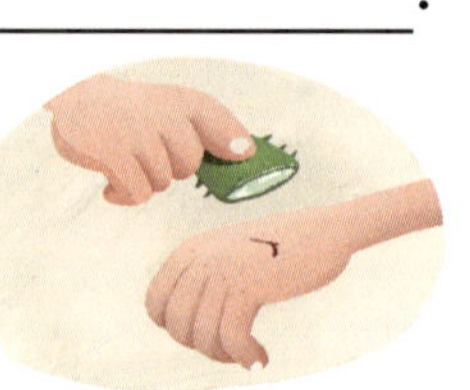

4  Some plants give us ___________.

- keep us warm　　• make a soft bed
- food to eat　　　• used as medicines

Grammar Connection

 **Fill in the blanks by using "verb + -(e)d."**

Use -**(e)d** at the ends of regular verbs to make the past tense.
ex She liked to hike. (like) / She climbed a big rock. (climb)

1 She ____________ some leaves as a blanket. (use)

2 Jen ____________ for an aloe vera plant. (look)

3 She ____________ some medicine. (need)

4 She ____________ to make a campfire. (decide)

5 She ____________ to hike. (love)

 **Fill in the graphic organizer.**

How Did Jungle Jen Solve Her Problems in the Jungle?

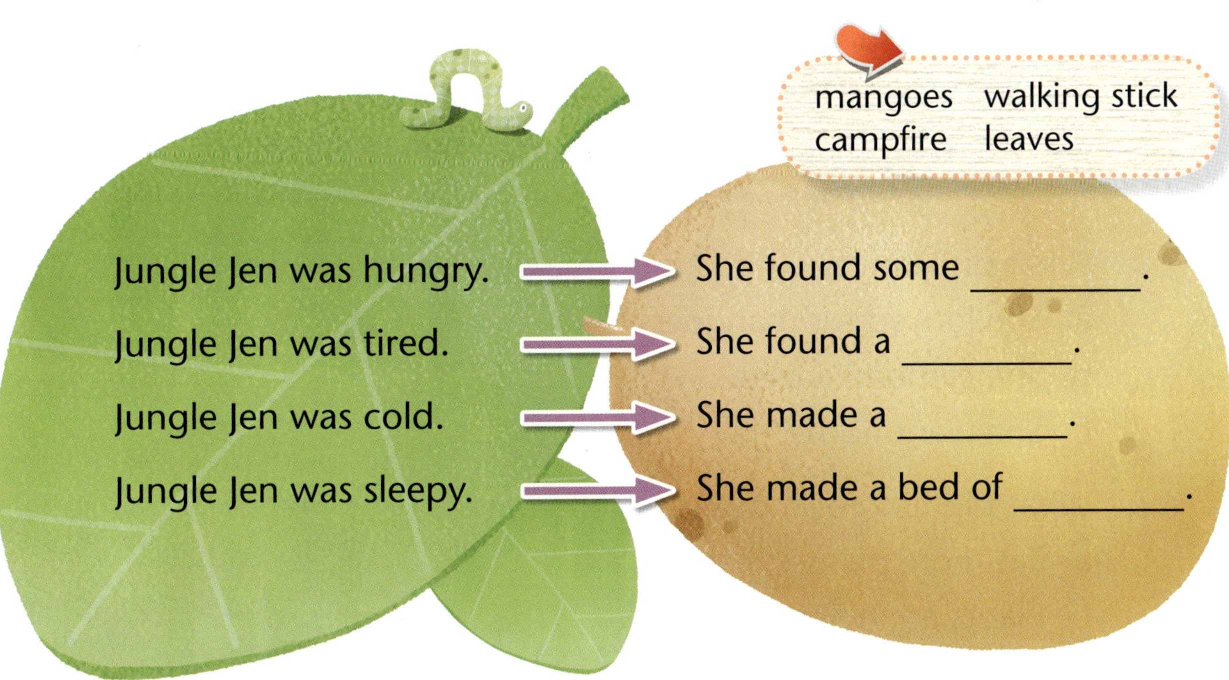

Wrap Up

A **Read the passage and answer the questions.**

> Ginseng is a root. It can help you in many ways. If you are tired or sick, have some ginseng. If you are cold, drink some ginseng tea. Your body will be warm. Many people eat and drink ginseng as medicine. Do you?

1 What is one way people do NOT use ginseng?
a. making paper with it   b. eating it
c. drinking it

2 If you are cold, how will ginseng help you?
a. It will make you less tired.   b. It will make you warm.
c. It will make you sleepy.

B **Read the story and answer the questions.**

> In the morning, Jungle Jen ate some bananas for breakfast. Then, she went home. Jungle Jen was so happy the plants in the jungle helped her. She wanted to tell other people about how helpful plants are. She wanted to say that it is important for us to help plants, too.

1 What did Jungle Jen do after breakfast?
a. She looked for mangoes.
b. She climbed a tree.
c. She went home.

2 What did Jungle Jen want to tell people?
a. Eat more plants.
b. Plants are helpful.
c. Hiking is fun.

Unique Food from around the World

Warm Up

- What's your favorite meal?
  What is it made from?
- What are some unique dishes?

Get Ready

A Match the words with the pictures.

bugs   insects   snacks   fried food   a mound of rice

B Choose the words to complete the sentences.

1. I hope my mom will (donate / decorate) my birthday cake.

2. Strawberry is my favorite (flavor / fruit) of ice cream.

3. Before you cook, you must prepare all the (ingredients / interests).

4. I (chip / dip) cookies in hot tea.

5. The apple is very (tough / crunchy).

What Unique Food!

Name: *Charlie*   **Date:** *May 7*
Instructions: *Write about some of the unique dishes that people eat around the world. Then, explain how they are cooked.*

I researched some unique dishes made with insects around the world.
5 They are as follows:

1. **Name of the Food: Deep Fried Tarantula**
   Country: Cambodia

In Cambodia, a popular dish is deep fried tarantula. Tarantulas are large spiders. They
10 are as big as an adult's palm. This food is a sweet snack that kids like. The spiders are fried in oil and sometimes are covered with sugar. At other times, they are dipped in salt. They taste like chicken and potato chips.

2. **Name of the Food:** *Crunchy Grasshopper*
Country: Thailand

In Thailand, people like eating crunchy
grasshoppers. The grasshoppers are
as long as a finger. First, they fry the
grasshoppers in oil. Then, garlic and
herbs are added for flavor. They are
crunchy and taste good.

3. **Name of the Food:** *Insect Sushi*
Country: *Japan*

In Japan, some people use many kinds
of insects to make a special sushi. They
carefully select insects like cockroaches,
bees, and scorpions. The insects are fried
in oil, and then they are put on a mound of rice. The crunchy
fried insects with the sweet and sour rice make a
wonderful taste.

People think insects are healthy and tasty. In fact, insects are full
of protein. These days, we have to raise lots of cows and pigs to get
protein. But we don't need to raise insects. They can be a perfect
food source. How about trying some insects as a special food?

Reading Skills

- **Main Idea**
  This story is mainly about (unique dishes / insects).
- **Searching for Information**
  Underline the sentences that give information about
  how to cook the unique dish in each country.

Comprehension Check Up

A **Check True or False.**

1 People never eat insects.　　　　　　　　T　F

2 A tarantula is a very small spider.　　　　T　F

3 Insects can be a great food source.　　　　T　F

B **Choose the correct answers.**

1 Cambodians enjoy tarantulas as a __________ .
   a. soup　　　　　　　b. snack　　　　　　　c. sushi

2 Grasshoppers can be a __________ and tasty food.
   a. salty　　　　　　　b. crunchy　　　　　　c. sweet

3 Why do people enjoy eating insects?
   a. Because they are cheap.
   b. Because people do not have any other food.
   c. Because they are healthy and tasty.

C **Fill in the table.**

Crunchy　insects　mound　garlic　Japan　spiders　grasshoppers　dip　Fried

Unique Food

Picture	Food	Country	How to Cook
	Deep ________ Tarantula	Cambodia	Fry the ________ in oil. Cover them with sugar or ________ them in salt.
	________ Grasshopper	Thailand	Fry the ________ in oil. Add ________ and herbs.
	Insect Sushi	________	Fry the ________ in oil. Put them on a ________ of rice.

Write the "plural nouns" in the blanks by using the words given.

> Add **-s** to make the plural forms of most countable nouns.
>
> Add **-es** to make the plural forms of nouns ending in s, sh, ch, or x.
>
> **ex** I like to play with my friends.
>
> There are many bugs in the bushes.

1 I researched some strange ____________. (dish)

2 Tarantulas are large ____________. (spider)

3 The ____________ are as long as a finger. (grasshopper)

4 The ____________ are fried in oil. (insect)

5 We have to raise ____________ on large areas of land. (cow)

On Your Own

Fill in the graphic organizer.

Unique Food from around the World

Insects   grasshoppers
perfect   sushi   spiders

Introduction

____________ are a unique food.

Body

Cambodians eat ____________ for snack.

Thais like to eat ____________.

Japanese use many kinds of insects for ____________.

Conclusion

Insects can be a ____________ food source.

Lunch with Mariko

Mariko was the nicest woman in our village. She always had a smile on her face. One day, she invited my friend
5 Thomas and me to lunch. We were excited. We wondered what she would cook.

We arrived for lunch at noon. "Welcome, boys. Lunch is almost ready," she said.
10 From the kitchen, we smelled fried food. It smelled great.

We watched Mariko cook. First, Mariko fried some things in oil. They were fat and brown. Next, she fried some large and black things. She put them on a mound of rice. They looked like sushi. Last, she decorated them with yellow and pink flowers and green leaves.

5 "Okay, boys. Try these first. If you like them, I'll make more," said Mariko.

We were both interested in trying them. I said, "Okay, Thomas. You eat the black one, and I'll eat the brown one. Are you ready? On the count of three: one, two, three."

10 Crunch! Squish! We both ate them. I looked at Thomas. I saw his eyes open wide. A large smile appeared on his face. He liked the sushi. And I liked it, too.

"So, boys, do you like them?" asked Mariko.

"More, please," we said.

15 "Sure! Let's get some ingredients for more food," said Mariko.

We followed Mariko outside. She walked to some green bushes. She picked up a large rock. Under the rock were

20 beetles, worms, and spiders. Mariko picked up the bugs and insects. Thomas and I were shocked. She had cooked them for lunch. Eww!

Reading Skills

- **Main Idea**
  This story is mainly about a special (lunch / woman).

- **Sequence**
  Underline the sentences that show the sequence of cooking.

A **Check True or False.**

1 Mariko was the nicest woman in the town. T F

2 Thomas did not want to try the food. T F

3 The boys liked the food before they knew what it was. T F

B **Choose the correct answers.**

1 Mariko invited the boys for ___________.
  a. breakfast   b. lunch   c. dinner

2 The food smelled ___________.
  a. great   b. terrible   c. sweet

3 How did the boys feel when they saw the ingredients?
  a. surprised   b. happy   c. excited

C **Fill in the graphic organizer.**

How Did Mariko Get Some Ingredients for Lunch?

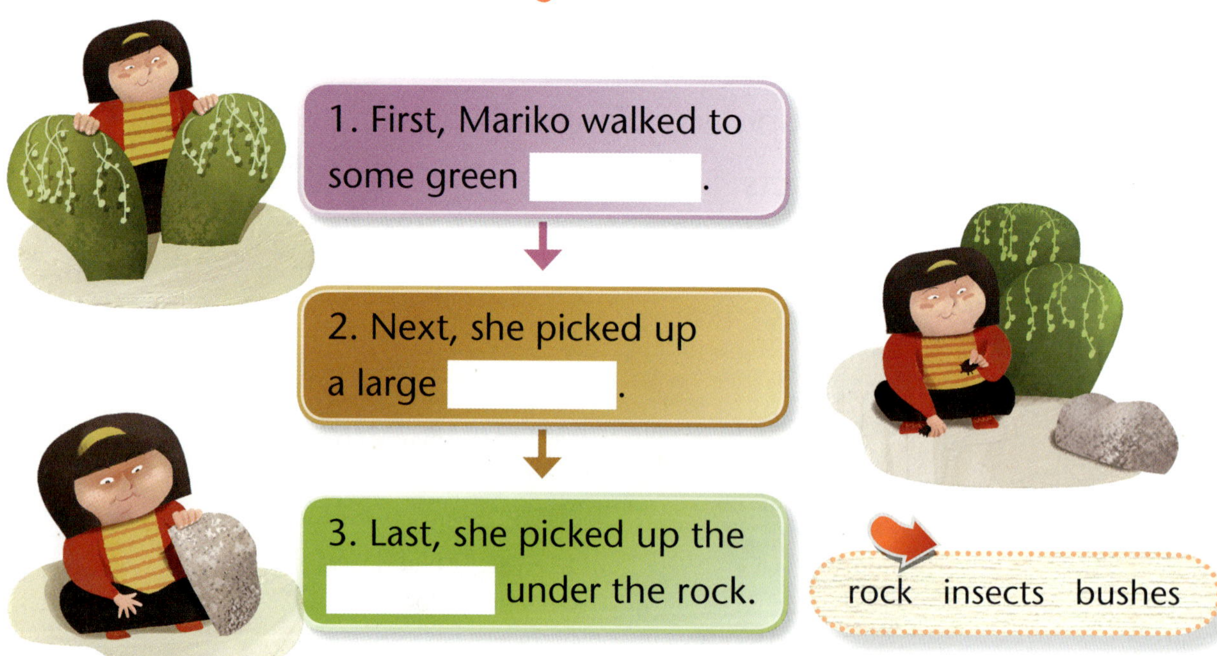

Grammar Connection

Check the correct positions to put the words given.

> An **adjective** is a word that describes a noun.
> Put the **adjective** before the noun to describe it.
> **ex** I eat a <u>red</u> apple. / He walks with his <u>cute</u> dog.

1 Mariko was a woman in our village. (nice)

2 She put it on a flower. (pink)

3 She decorated them with insects. (strange)

4 I'll eat the one. (brown)

5 She walked to some bushes. (green)

On Your Own

Fill in the blanks in the correct order.

How Did Mariko Cook Lunch?

1 She ____________ some things ____________.

2 She put them on a ____________ of rice.

3 She ____________ them with flowers and leaves.

A Read the passage and answer the questions.

In America, a popular treat is a Hotlix. A Hotlix is a scorpion lollipop. You can buy them in many flavors such as banana, apple, and blueberry. First, you enjoy sucking on the flavored candy. Then, when you have finished the candy, you can eat the scorpion. For only 3 dollars, you can enjoy a special scorpion lollipop.

1 Where are scorpion lollipops popular?
a. Austria　　　　　b. America　　　　　c. Cambodia

2 What can you do when you finish the candy?
a. throw it away　　　b.eat the scorpion　　c. pay 3 dollars

B Read the story and answer the questions.

Thomas and I followed Mariko back into the kitchen. We didn't like the idea of eating insects, but we did like their taste.
"So what will you have this time, boys?" asked Mariko.
"I'd like to try a beetle," Thomas answered.
"And I'd like to try a worm," I said. "But this time, no flowers, please. Only the worm."
"Only the worm?" asked Mariko. "Eww!"

1 What did the boys like about eating insects?
a. the idea of it　　　b. the taste　　　　c. the kind of bugs

2 What did Thomas want to eat?
a. a beetle　　　　　b. a worm　　　　　c. a spider

An Amazing Story

Warm Up

- Do you know any amazing stories?
- Do you know anyone amazing?

Get Ready

A Match the words with the pictures.

trick   dolphin   plastic   aquarium   whistle

B Choose the words to complete the sentences.

1. Dolphins are (amazing / shocking) animals. 

2. An alligator (scoops / swallows) a small fish.

3. He is (smart / short) because he passed
   the difficult test.

4. Open your mouth. I'll (remove / repair) the fishbone.

5. Help, help! Please (save / say) me.   

Lucky Dolphins

Do you want to hear an **amazing** story?
It all began in the town of Fushun, China. Two **dolphins** were swimming in an **aquarium**. There was **plastic** in the pool, and they **swallowed** some. But the dolphins couldn't digest
5 the plastic. The plastic hurt their stomachs. Soon, they stopped eating their food. The workers were worried. They tried to **remove** the plastic from their stomachs. But they failed. The dolphins became very weak. If the plastic could not be removed, the dolphins would die.

One of the workers had an idea. He remembered Bao Xishun, the
10 world's tallest man. He was 2.36 meters tall, and his arms were 1.06 meters long. The worker thought that Bao could **save** the dolphins. He could reach inside the dolphins' stomachs with his long arms. Then, he could take out the plastic. The worker called Bao, and he agreed to help

save the dolphins. Workers opened the dolphins' mouths. Then, they wrapped towels around the dolphins' teeth. Now the dolphins' teeth couldn't hurt Bao. With his long arms, Bao reached inside the dolphins' stomachs. He took out the plastic. Bao saved the dolphins.

Today, the dolphins are happy again. Many people come to see them in their aquarium. And it is all thanks to the world's tallest man. What an amazing story!

- **Main Idea**
  This story is mainly about saving the (dolphins / aquarium).
- **Problem and Solution**
  Circle the sentences that show the problem.
  Underline the sentences that show the solution.

Comprehension Check Up

A **Check True or False.**

1 This story took place in China.   T F

2 Two dolphins swallowed some plastic.   T F

3 The dolphins could digest the plastic.   T F

B **Choose the correct answers.**

1 The world's tallest man has long ___________.
   a. arms   b. hair   c. nails

2 The workers wrapped the dolphins' teeth, so they couldn't ________.
   a. breathe   b. hurt the tallest man   c. save the tallest man

3 What did the tallest man remove from the dolphins' stomachs?
   a. small fish   b. plastic   c. their teeth

C **Fill in the graphic organizer.**

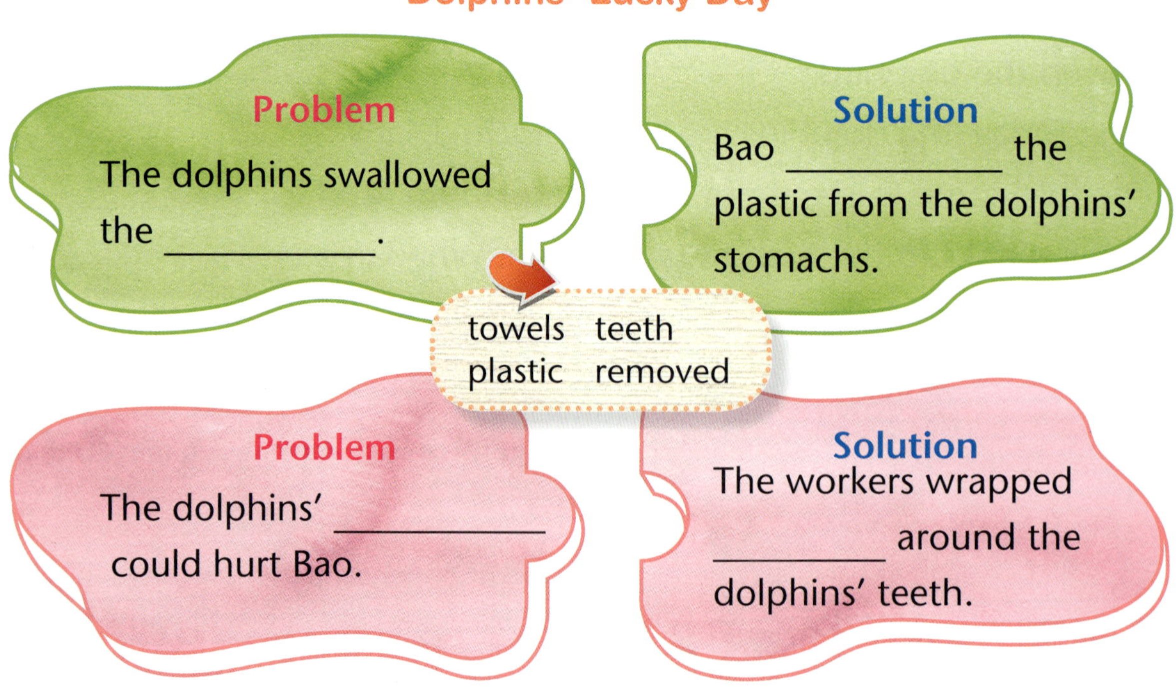

Grammar Connection

Divide each sentence into two parts by using a slash(/).

A sentence has two parts: a **subject** and a **predicate**.
ex Tom / swims in the pool.
The two boys / like to play soccer.

1 Two dolphins were swimming in an aquarium.

2 The plastic hurt their stomachs.

3 The workers were worried.

4 Then, he could take out the plastic.

5 The dolphins' teeth couldn't hurt Bao.

Fill in the blanks in the correct order.

Dolphins in Trouble

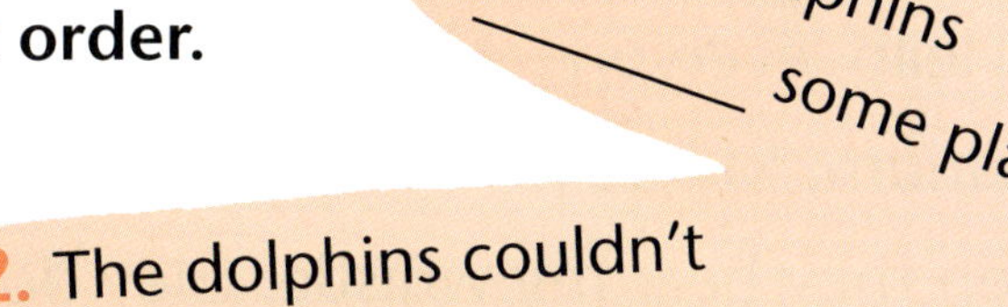

eating   hurt   weak
digest   swallowed

Those Amazing Dolphins!

Hello, everyone. My name is Dave. I am a dolphin trainer at this aquarium. My dolphins are very smart. I trained them with my whistle. When they hear my whistle, they do tricks. Watch. Tweet! The dolphins come to my side. Tweet, tweet! They wave their flippers at you.
5 Everyone, say hello to my lovely dolphins.

I also trained my dolphins to read. I will show them this card. My lovely dolphins, read the words on this card.

> Jump high in the air
> and do a backflip.

10 Now, show me the trick. Watch the dolphins swim off like a flash of lightning. Look how they jump high in the air and do a backflip.

Everyone, are you enjoying the show? This time, I will not blow
my whistle. Shh! Everybody, this will be my dolphins' best trick. I need
a volunteer. Over there! The boy with a red shirt. What about you?
Can you write some tricks on this card? Thank you! Shh~~! This time,
I will not show it to the dolphins. Dolphins, show us the tricks that are
written on the card. Look! They jump through two hoops. Wait. Where
are they going? They're coming straight at me. They
jump high in the air... Splash! Oh, my gosh! They soak
me with water. Let's look at the card.

> Jump through two hoops.
> Then, soak Dave with water.

Look! They did the tricks without reading
the card. Oh, those amazing
dolphins!

Reading Skills

- **Main Idea**
  This story is mainly about (a trainer / training dolphins).
- **Sequence**
  Underline the sentences that show the sequence of tricks.

Comprehension Check Up

A **Check True or False.**

1 Dave is a dolphin trainer.   T   F

2 The dolphins can read tricks.   T   F

3 Dolphins cannot be trained.   T   F

B **Choose the correct answers.**

1 The dolphins do ___________ according to the trainer's instructions.
   a. shouting   b. showers   c. tricks

2 What trick do the dolphins perform after hearing two whistles?
   a. They swim below the pool.   b. They wave their flippers.
   c. They jump through two hoops.

3 What cannot the dolphins understand?
   a. words   b. whistles   c. colors

C **Fill in the blanks with the words from the box.**

backflip
side
hoops
flippers

What Tricks Can the Dolphins Do?

1 The dolphins come to Dave's __________.

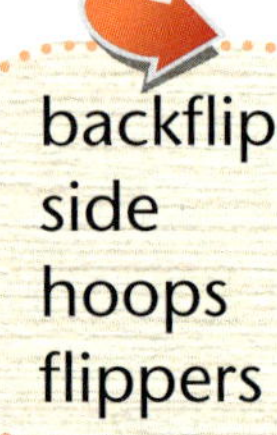

2   The dolphins wave their __________.

3 The dolphins jump high in the air and do a __________.

4   The dolphins jump through two __________ and splash Dave with water.

Grammar Connection

Underline the "simple subject" and "simple predicate" in each sentence.

> The **simple subject** is the main word in the subject.
> The **simple predicate** is the main word in the predicate.
> **ex** My <u>name</u> <u>is</u> Jane. / <u>I</u> <u>study</u> math in the room.

1 Some trainers work at this aquarium.

2 The handsome man trained them with his whistle.

3 The smart dolphins swim off again.

4 They jump high in the air.

5 The crowd cheers even louder this time.

On Your Own

Fill in the main idea and details.

Why Are the Dolphins _________?

read   tricks
whistle   Amazing

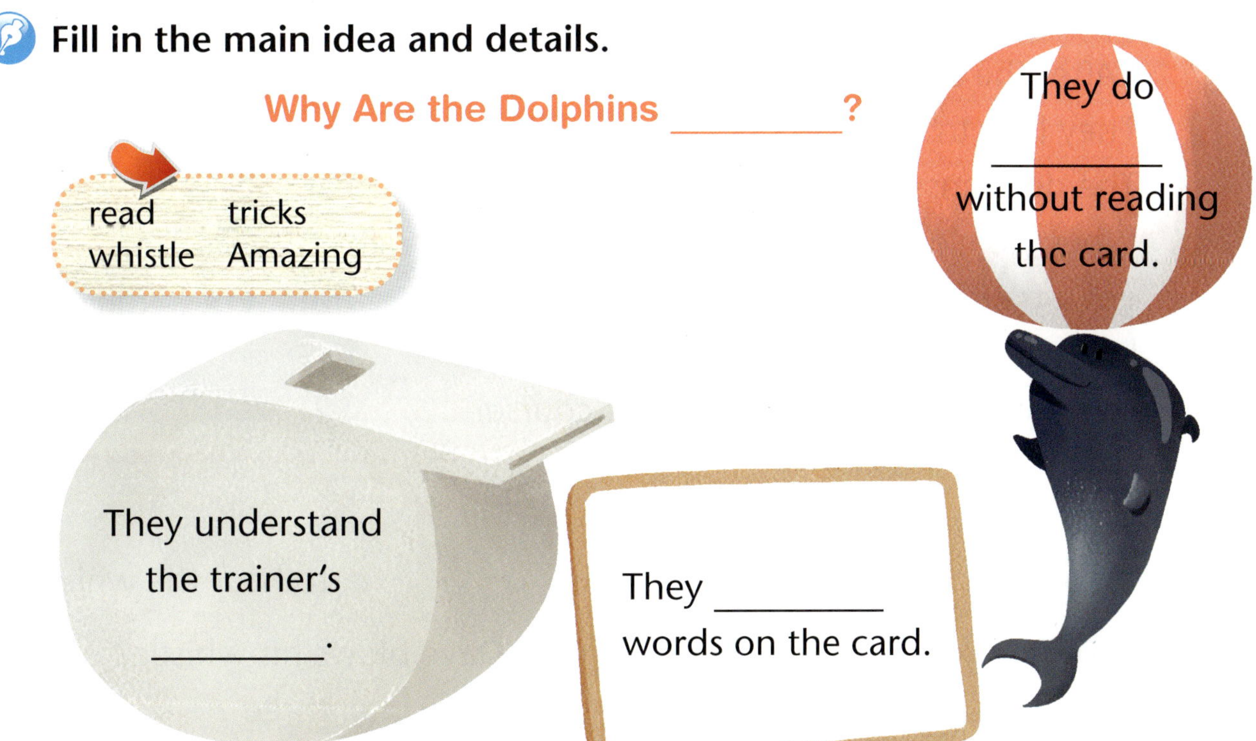

Wrap Up

A **Read the passage and answer the questions.**

> Would you believe Bao was not the first tall man to save some dolphins? In 1978, American basketball player Clifford Ray saved a dolphin at a California aquarium. The dolphin swallowed a piece of metal and was in danger of dying. Clifford used his 1.14-meter-long arms to reach into the dolphin's stomach and take out the metal. He saved the dolphin.

1 What did the dolphin in California swallow?

a. plastic   b. metal   c. a fish

2 With what did Clifford save the dolphin?

a. his long foot   b. his long neck   c. his long arms

B **Read the story and answer the questions.**

> After the show, Dave gives the dolphins their treats. They love to get treats. That is how Dave trains them. The dolphins will do a trick, so they can get a treat. When he blows his whistle, they know they will get a treat. When they read the cards, they know they will get four treats. Can you guess what their treat is? Fish, of course!

1 Why do the dolphins do tricks?

a. to be famous   b. to get fish   c. to hear the whistle

2 How many fish will the dolphins get if Dave blows his whistle?

a. one   b. two   c. three

Beyond Words

Warm Up

- What do these hand gestures mean?
- When do you use them?

Get Ready

A Match the words with the pictures.

slap   sword   hand gestures   stadium   spear

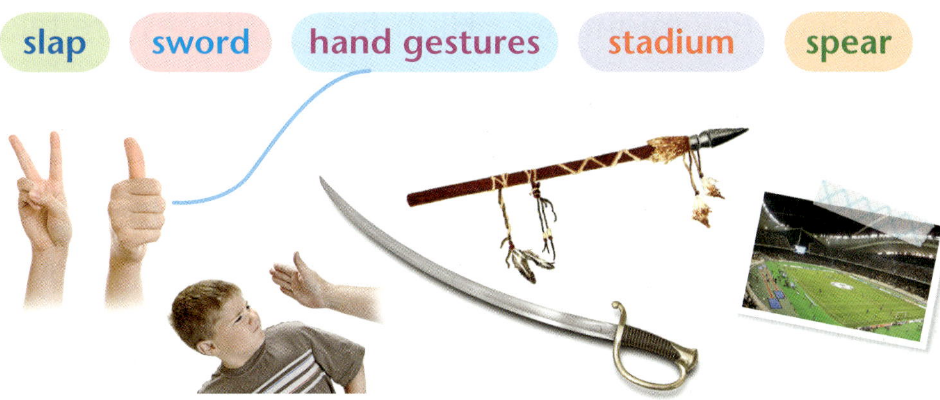

B Choose the words to complete the sentences.

1. Sophie is a (positive / negative) person, so she smiles all the time.

2. The brave (gladiator / glider) won the fight.

3. The (pianist / audience) enjoy the show.

4. She came to (surprise / celebrate) my baby's first birthday.

5. We (communicate / raise) by phone and email.

HAND GESTURES

Sometimes you use hand gestures such as a high five or an okay sign. When do you use them? Why do you use them? What are their meanings, and where do they come from?

Two boys raise their hands and head high. Then they hit their
5 palms together. They might say, "High-five." This gesture takes its
name from the five fingers on a hand and the raising of hands high.
The first high five was done in 1977 at a baseball stadium in America.
When a Los Angeles baseball player hit a homerun, another player
raised his hand to slap the player's hand in celebration. Now, people
10 use this gesture to celebrate something.

A cute girl shows thumbs up. She closes her
fists with her thumbs upward. Thumbs up means
"well done" or "good job" and is a positive sign. This gesture comes
from the audience in the ancient Roman Coliseum. The audience voted
5   on the life or death of a defeated gladiator. A thumbs up gave life, and
a thumbs down gave death.

The scuba diver in the water gives the okay sign by making a circle
with two fingers. When you're eating food, it's impolite to talk with
your mouth full. In that case, you can use it to mean "great" or "fine."
10   Hand gestures are a good way to
communicate. Hand gestures can mean
more than the words you speak. Think of
some other gestures that you sometimes
use. What do you think they mean? Where
15   do they come from?

Reading Skills

• **Main Idea**
This story is mainly about (hand gestures /
body gestures).

• **Describing**
Underline the sentences that describe the
pictures.

Comprehension Check Up

A **Check True or False.**

1 To celebrate something, people give high fives. T F

2 People communicate only with words. T F

3 The thumbs-up gesture comes from ancient Greece. T F

B **Choose the correct answers.**

1 This story does NOT tell about the ___________.
   a. thumbs up   b. high five   c. stop sign

2 Which hand gesture can you do to show "great" during a meal?
   a. the high five   b. the thumbs up   c. the okay sign

3 Why do people use hand gestures?
   a. They are polite.   b. They mean more than words.
   c. They do not have any meanings.

C **Fill in the graphic organizer.**

When Do People Use Hand Gestures?

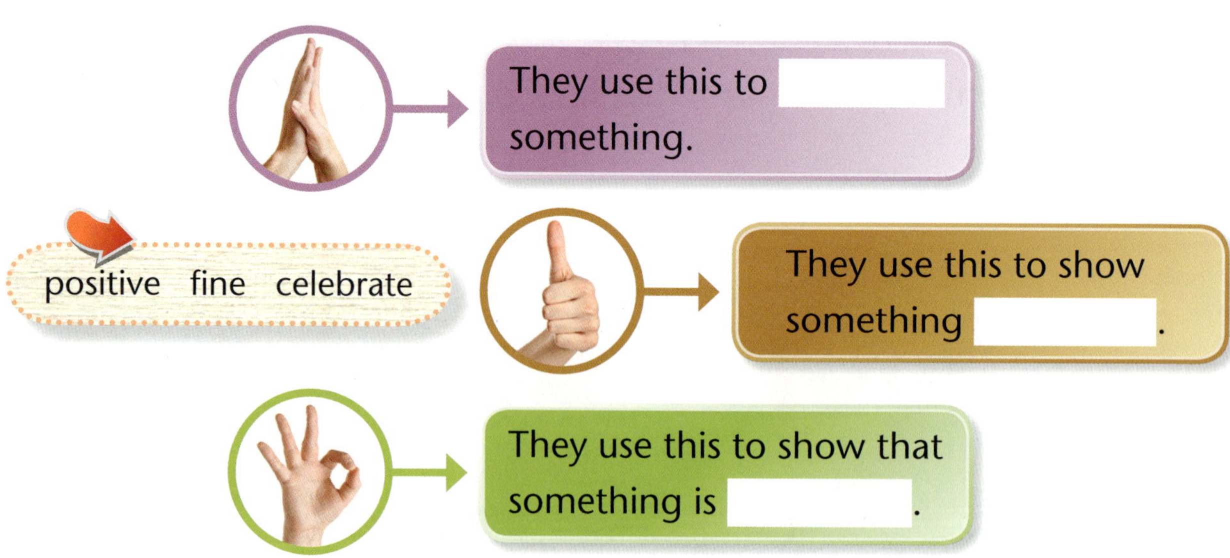

Grammar Connection

Fill in the blanks to make questions.

> Use **Wh** questions with words such as **who, what, when, where, why, which,** and **how** to ask or make questions.
>
> **ex** <u>Who</u> is the girl in the photo?
> <u>What</u> do you want to eat for lunch?

1 _____________ do you use them? Tell me the time.

2 _____________ do you use them? Tell me the reason.

3 _____________ do you use them? Tell me the way.

4 _____________ do they come from? Tell me the place.

5 _____________ do you think it is? Tell me the meaning.

 On Your Own

Fill in the chart.

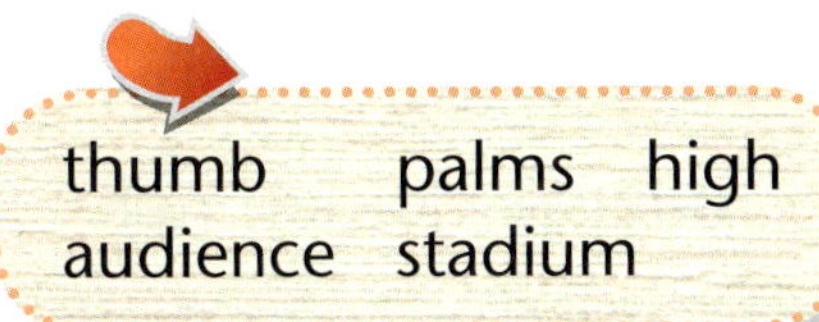

Which Hand Gestures Do You Prefer?

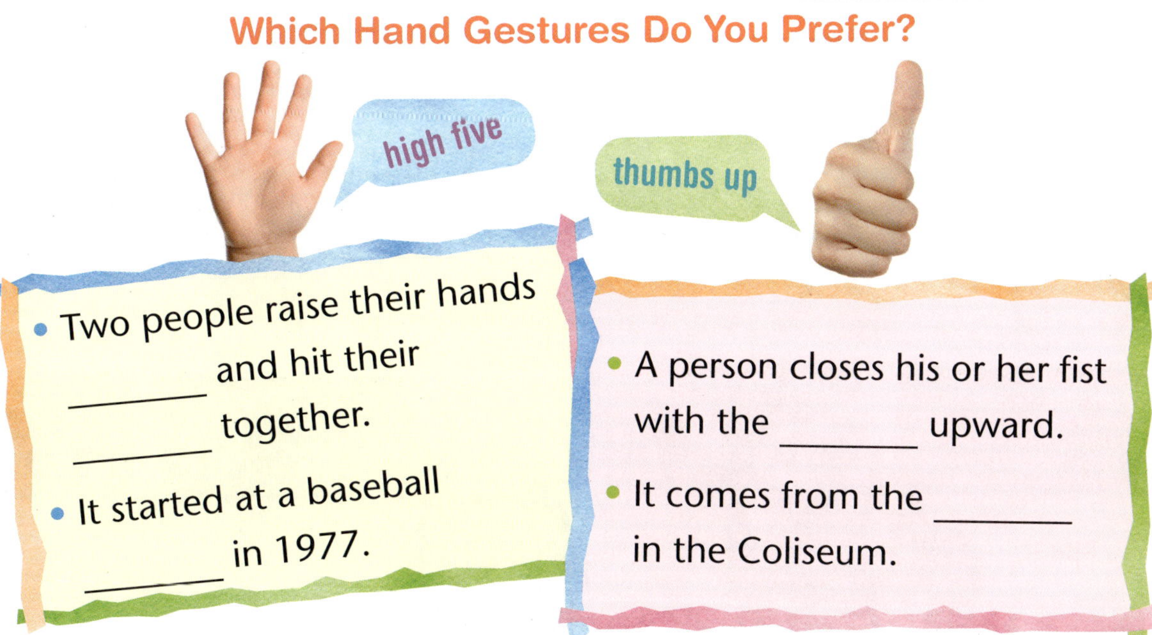

A Day at the Coliseum

"Hey, Marcus," I shout. "Hurry up. Or we are going to miss the fight."

My best friend Marcus and I are going to the Coliseum. We are going to see the gladiators fight. I don't want to be late. There are so
5   many people that we have to push our way through the crowd. There are even Roman soldiers there. They are saluting each other.

Finally, we arrive. We look down at the gladiators. They are so big. And they look very strong.

"Wow, Antony," says Marcus. "Look at Spartacus over there. He has
10   a large golden helmet on his head. In his hand, he has a sharp sword. I hope he wins."

"No way," I tell Marcus. "I like Maximus. He has a silver mask on his face. In his hand, he has a long spear. I hope he wins."

The fight begins. Both gladiators fight well. The crowd is cheering. They are enjoying the fight. Marcus and I are enjoying the fight, too.

5　Soon, the fight is over. Spartacus, with the golden helmet, fought very well. He won the fight. Now, both gladiators stand in the middle of the Coliseum. They are waiting for the audience to decide if Maximus lives or dies.

Suddenly, everyone in the audience begins to cheer.
10　Marcus and I cheer, too. Then, we all give the thumbs-up gesture. Maximus fought well. We want him to live.

Walking home, Marcus and I are happy. What a great day
15　at the Coliseum!

Spartacus and Maximus are both great gladiators. I wonder who will win the next time.

Main Idea
This story is mainly about the fighting in the (Coliseum / college).

Details
Underline the sentences that show what the gladiators use to fight.

A **Check True or False.**

1 Antony and Marcus see the gladiators fight.   T   F

2 There are not many people at the Coliseum.   T   F

3 Both gladiators fought well.   T   F

B **Choose the correct answers.**

1 What were the Roman soldiers doing outside the Coliseum?
   a. fighting   b. watching   c. saluting

2 Which gladiator does Antony want to win?
   a. Maximus   b. Spartacus   c. Marcus

3 Why does the audience give the gladiators the thumbs-up gesture?
   a. Maximus didn't fight well.   b. Maximus fought well.
   c. Nobody fought well.

C **Fill in the graphic organizer.**

Roman Gladiators

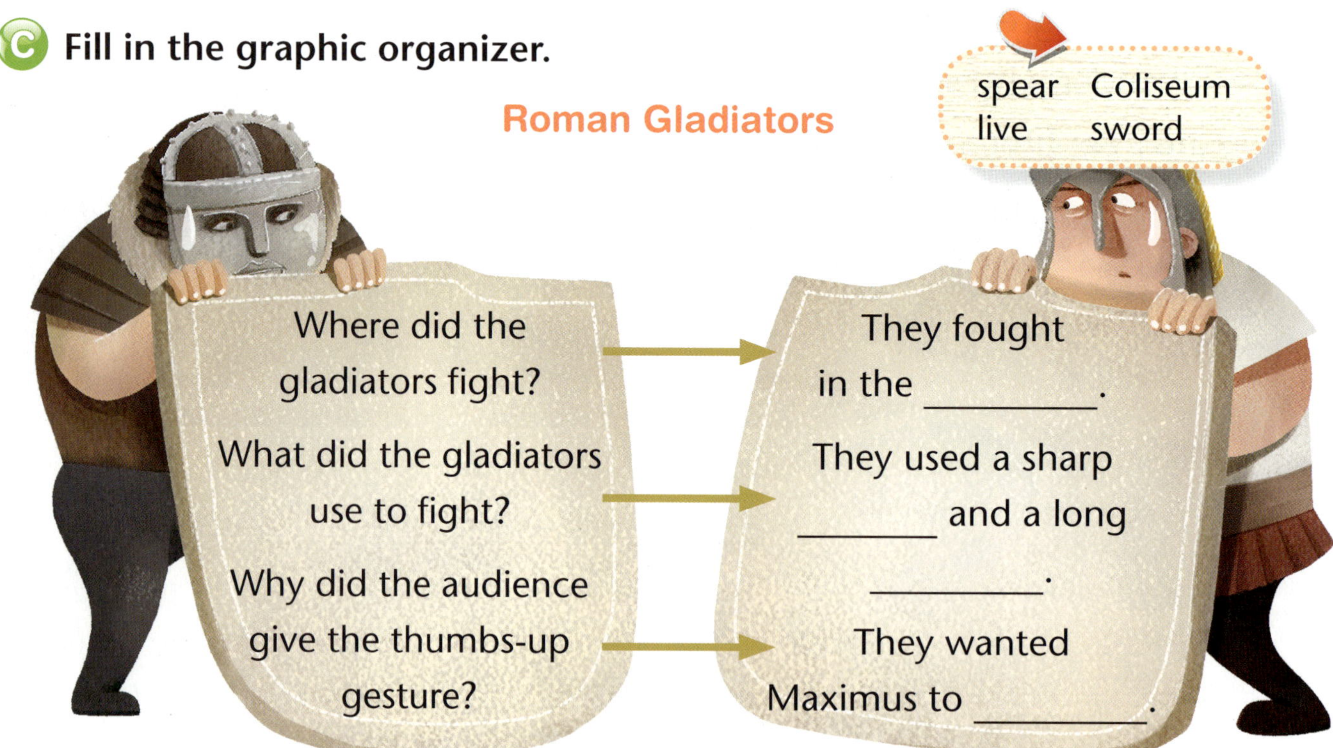

Grammar Connection

Write the present continuous tense forms of the words given.

> Use **be + verb-ing** to make the present continuous tense.
> **ex** We <u>are learning</u> English. (learn)
> She <u>is making</u> a delicious cake for her kids. (make)

1 Marcus and I ___________________ to the Coliseum. (go)

2 He ___________________ the gladiators fight. (watch)

3 They ___________________ each other. (salute)

4 The crowd ___________________. (cheer)

5 They ___________________ the fight. (enjoy)

 On Your Own

 Fill in the blanks in the correct order.

A Day at the Coliseum

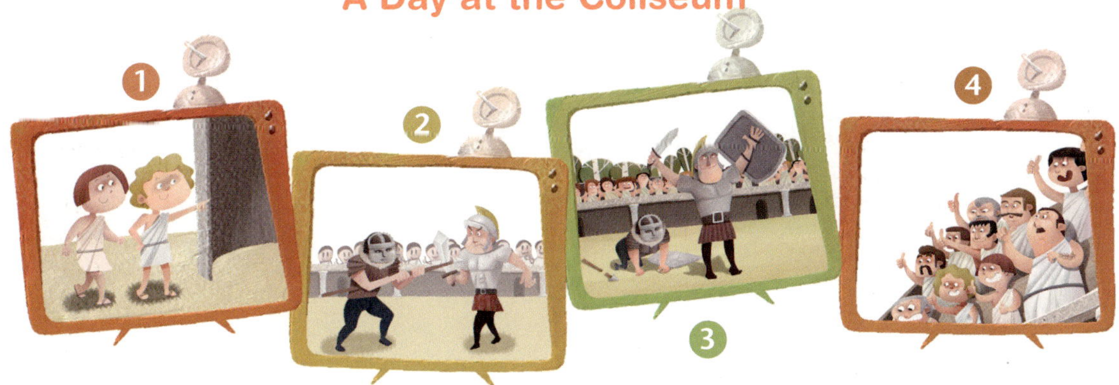

1 Marcus and Antony are going to see the ___________ fight.

2 Spartacus and Maximus ___________ fight well.

3 Spartacus ___________ the fight.

4 The audience gives the ___________ gesture to Maximus.

Wrap Up

A Read the passage and answer the questions.

> The girl makes the V gesture. She makes her hand into a fist. Then, she raises and parts her middle and index fingers. The V gesture has different meanings. This gesture means victory and peace. People also use it when they have their pictures taken. Do you use this gesture?

1 What does the girl do with her fingers?
a. makes a circle with them　　b. raises and parts them
c. raises and hits them

2 What is NOT a meaning of this gesture?
a. victory　　　b. peace　　　c. goodbye

B Read the story and answer the questions.

> At home, Marcus and I pretend we are gladiators. Our swords bang together, and we jump around the house. Finally, the fight is over. We pretend we hear the audience cheering. Then, when the audience gives the thumbs up, we jump high in the air. We high-five each other and yell, "Hooray."

1 What do the boys do at home?
a. They pretend they are the audience.
b. They walk around the house.
c. They pretend they are gladiators.

2 At the end of the story, why do they high-five each other?
a. to celebrate　　b. to say, "Great job."　c. to say, "Goodbye."

Science inside Balls

Warm Up

- What sports are these balls for?
  How do you use them?
- Which ball is your favorite? Why?

Get Ready

A **Match the words with the pictures.**

pitcher   fuzz   bumps   stitches   uniform

B **Choose the words to complete the sentences.**

1. He kicks the ball in the (direction / reaction) of the net.

2. The (surface / shirt) of the field has a lot of grass.

3. A boy (catches / bounces) a ball up and down on the ground.

4. I have ten (teammates / roommates) on my soccer team.

5. The player (grips / passes) the ball in his hands.

Missing Balls

Hi, everyone.

I lost my bag with four balls. Have you seen my balls? If you have seen them, please give them to me. They are my balls.

5 My basketball is big and orange. When you hold it, it feels bumpy. My baseball is small, hard, and white. When you throw it, you can feel the stitches on it. My tennis ball is small, soft, and yellow. When you hold it, it feels fuzzy. Last, my soccer ball is big and round. When you kick my soccer ball, it feels

10 hard.

I love my balls a lot. Please find my balls.

Thank you,

From Steven

Hi, Steven.

I found your bag on the playground. But I am wondering about your balls. Can you answer my questions in the spaces below?

5   Question **1**   Your basketball has small bumps on its surface. Why?
▶ *The small bumps help you grip the ball well. Basketball players grip it in their hand and throw it into the net.*

Question **2**   Your baseball has red stitches on it. Why?
▶ *The stitches on a baseball help it curve and change direction in the air. Pitchers can throw the baseball*
10
wherever they want.

Question **3**   Your tennis ball has a fuzzy surface. Why?
▶ *The fuzz on a tennis ball helps the ball bounce on a racket. Tennis players can bounce and spin the ball well*
15
with a racket.

If you write your answers in the spaces correctly, I will leave your balls at the lost and found.

20   From Russell

• **Main Idea**
This story is mainly about the (reasons / choices) that balls are different.

• **Details**
Circle the sentences that show the reason of the different looks of the balls.

Comprehension Check Up

A Check True or False.

1 A tennis ball is fuzzy.　　　　　　　　　　T　F

2 Basketballs are big and bumpy.　　　　　T　F

3 You can feel the stitches in a soccer ball.　T　F

B Choose the correct answers.

1 This story does NOT tell about how balls ___________.
   a. feel　　　　　　　　b. are alike　　　　　　c. look

2 Why do the balls look different?
   a. Balls come from different places.
   b. Balls come in different sizes.
   c. Balls are used in different ways.

3 Why can basketball players grip the ball well?
   a. There are small bumps on its surface.
   b. There are fuzzy hairs on its surface.
   c. There are stitches in the ball.

C Fill in the graphic organizer.

Why Do Balls Look Different?

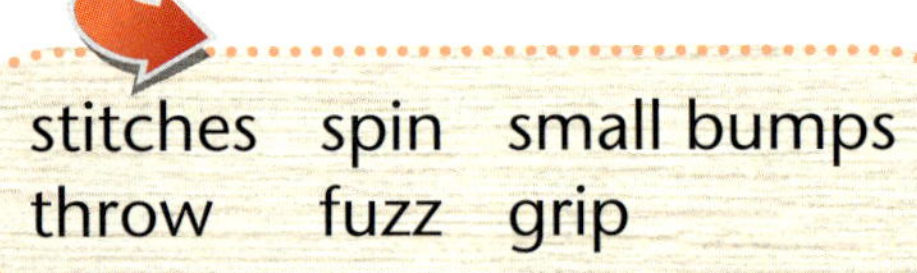

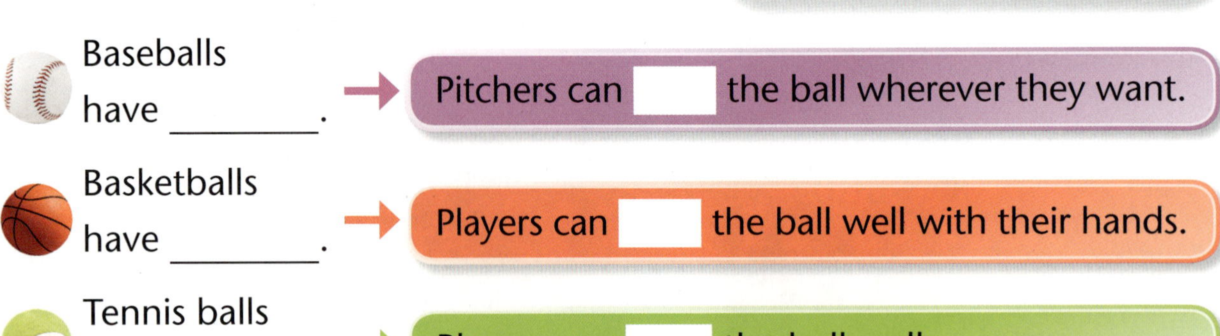

Baseballs have ________.　→　Pitchers can [ ] the ball wherever they want.

Basketballs have ________.　→　Players can [ ] the ball well with their hands.

Tennis balls have ________.　→　Players can [ ] the ball well.

Fill in the blanks by using "when" as a conjunction.

> Use **when** to connect the sentences as a conjunction.
> **ex** <u>When</u> you play basketball, put on your uniform.
> <u>When</u> you hit the ball, run to the first base.

1 ______________ you hold a basketball, it feels bumpy.

2 ______________ you throw a baseball, you can feel the stitches on it.

3 A tennis ball feels fuzzy ______________ you hold it.

4 ______________ you kick a soccer ball, it feels hard.

5 You feel happy ______________ you score a goal.

Fill in the Venn diagram.

A Closer Look at Two Balls

small bumps   hard
stitches   orange

It is big and ______.

It has ______ on its surface to help players grip the ball.

You play sports with them.

It is small, ______, and white.

It has ______ to help pitchers throw it wherever they want.

Basketball

Baseball

Game Day

Scott plays on a soccer team. He is getting ready for a game today. First, Scott puts on his blue uniform. Then, he puts on his soccer shoes. Next, he gets his bag. Last, he gets his soccer ball. Oh no! He cannot find his soccer ball.

5   Scott looks on top of the shelf. His ball is not there. Scott looks behind the door, next to the locker, and under the bench. It is not in those places either. Scott is feeling worried. Where could it be? Suddenly, Scott has an idea. He looks inside his bag. Aha! There is his ball. Now, he can go to the game.

The soccer game starts with the whistle. "Hey, over here," calls
Scott. He wants the ball. His teammate passes him the ball. The ball is
high in the air. Scott uses his head to bounce the ball into the net. It is
a goal!

5　　　"Yay," yells Scott.

The score is 1-0. They can win the game.

Scott has the ball. He runs toward the net.

"Kick! Kick!" yell Scott's teammates. But he does not kick the ball to
the net because the goalkeeper is ready to catch the ball. Scott passes
10　the ball to a teammate. Now, the goalkeeper cannot catch the ball.
Scott's teammate kicks the ball into the net. Now, the score is 2-0.

"Hooray, we won," yells Scott.

The game is over. Scott and his teammates
are happy to win the game.

15　　　Today is a wonderful day.

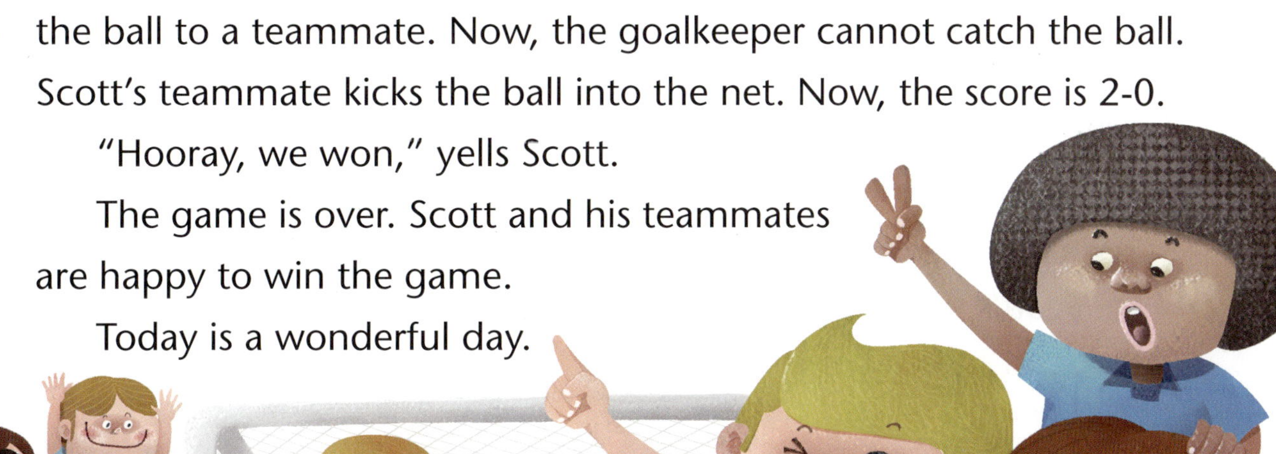

- **Main Idea**
  This story is mainly about playing (basketball /
  soccer).
- **Problem and Solution**
  Circle the sentences that show the problem.
  Underline the sentences that show the solution.

Comprehension Check Up

A **Check True or False.**

1 Scott finds his ball inside his bag. T F

2 Scott's uniform is red. T F

3 Scott looks on top of the shelf to find his ball. T F

B **Choose the correct answers.**

1 Scott is a good ___________.
a. player   b. student   c. pitcher

2 Scott's team scored ___________.
a. no goals   b. one goal   c. two goals

3 What happens at the end of the story?
a. Scott's team wins the game.   b. Scott's team loses the game.
c. Scott's team ties the game.

C **Fill in the blanks with the phrases from the box.**

What Happens on Game Day?

- gets his soccer ball
- puts on his uniform
- wins the game
- plays a soccer game

1 First, he ____________________.

2 Next, he ____________________.

3 Then, he ____________________.

4 Last, he ____________________.

Grammar Connection

 **Fill in the blanks by using the words "can" and "cannot."**

> Use **can** when somebody has the ability to do something.
> Use **cannot** when somebody doesn't have the ability to do something.
>
> **ex** The goalkeeper is ready. He <u>can</u> catch the ball.
> The goalkeeper is not ready. He <u>cannot</u> catch the ball.

1 He finds the ball. He ___________ go to the game.

2 He wants the ball. He ___________ score a goal.

3 The ball is high in the air. He ___________ kick the ball.

4 There is still time left. They ___________ win the game.

5 The goalkeeper is ready to catch the ball. Scott ___________ score.

 **Fill in the graphic organizer.**

How Does Scott Solve the Problem?

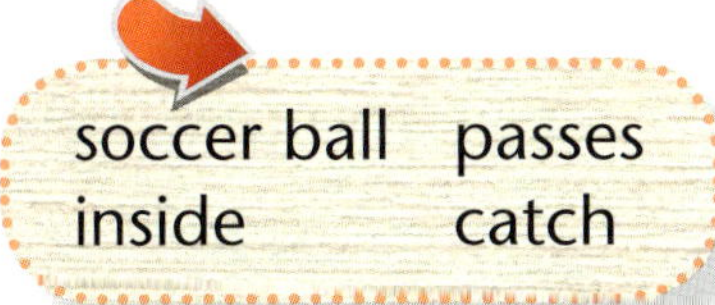

Problem → **Solution**

 He cannot find his ________. → He looks ________ his bag.

Problem → **Solution**

The goalkeeper is ready to ________ the ball. → Scott ________ the ball to a teammate.

A Read the passage and answer the questions.

> Many people like to play golf. When people play golf, they use a golf ball. A golf ball is small, hard, and white. It has small dimples all over its surface. When you hold a golf ball, it feels bumpy. Do you know why a golf ball feels bumpy? When a golfer hits the ball, the small dimples help it fly far through the air.

1 What does a golf ball have all over its surface?

a. hard hair　　　　b. small dimples　　　　c. white stitches

2 What do you do with a golf ball when you play golf?

a. hit it　　　　b. throw it　　　　c. bounce it

B Read the story and answer the questions.

> After the game, Scott and his teammates have a party. They feel great. They are talking about the game. "You did a great job using your head to score that goal!" says a teammate. "Thank you, " says Scott. "But we won together as a team. I am sure we can win every game as long as we help each other."

1 How do Scott and his teammates feel?

a. happy　　　　b. sad　　　　c. scared

2 How can Scott's team win every game?

a. by having a party　　　　b. by helping each other

c. by talking about the game

Answers

So Many Super Senses!

너무나 많은 뛰어난 감각들!

p.13

Get Ready

A

catfish whisker falcon antennae mosquito

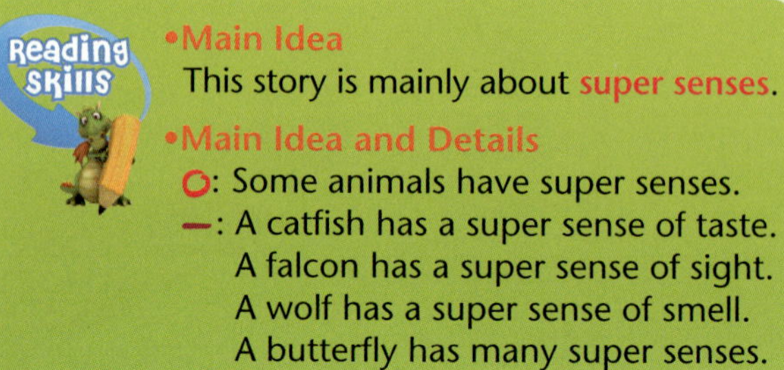

B 1. super sense 2. sticky 3. superhero
4. cape 5. yell

- **Main Idea**
  This story is mainly about **super senses**.
- **Main Idea and Details**
  O: Some animals have super senses.
  —: A catfish has a super sense of taste.
  A falcon has a super sense of sight.
  A wolf has a super sense of smell.
  A butterfly has many super senses.

Comprehension Check Up

(A) 1. F   2. F   3. T
(B) 1. b   2. b   3. c
(C) 1. tastes   2. hears   3. smells
4. sees

Grammar Connection

1. doesn't   2. does   3. don't
4. do   5. Does

On Your Own

Animal's Super Senses

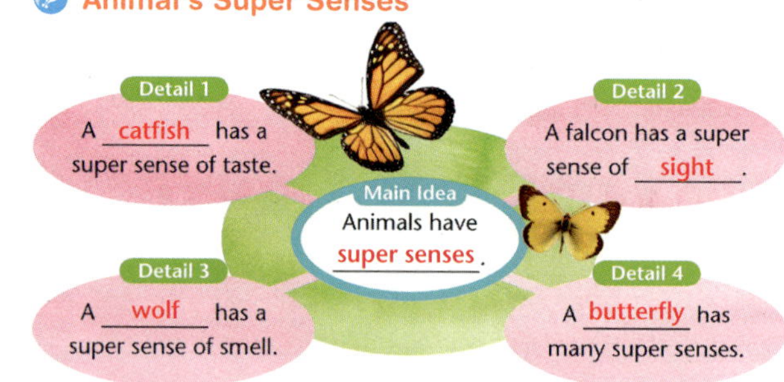

Lesson 1

p.14

Animals with Super Senses

뛰어난 감각을 가진 동물들

어떤 동물들은 뛰어난 감각을 가지고 있어요. 그들의 감각은 우리보다 훨씬 더 뛰어나지요.

여러분은 혀로 맛을 느껴요. 여러분은 온몸으로 맛을 느낄 수 있나요? 메기는 몸 전체로 맛을 느껴요. 메기는 심지어 수염으로도 맛을 느끼죠. 메기는 뛰어난 미각을 가지고 있어요.

여러분은 눈으로 보지요. 얼마나 멀리 볼 수 있나요? 여러분은 작은 쥐를 10 미터 밖에서 볼 수 있지요. 매는 똑같은 쥐를 1,500 미터 밖에서도 볼 수 있답니다. 매는 뛰어난 시각을 지니고 있어요.

여러분은 코로 냄새를 맡아요. 여러분은 10 미터 밖에서 바비큐 그릴에서 요리되는 고기의 냄새를 맡을 수 있어요. 늑대는 고기 냄새를 1,000 미터 밖에서도 맡을 수 있답니다. 늑대는 뛰어난 후각을 가지고 있어요.

나비는 뛰어난 감각을 많이 가지고 있어요. 나비는 겹눈을 가지고 있어요. 머리를 돌리지 않고도 모든 방향을 볼 수 있답니다. 나비는 뛰어난 시각을 지니고 있지요. 나비는 코가 없어요. 그러면 어떻게 냄새를 맡을까요? 나비는 더듬이로 냄새를 맡아요. 나비는 뛰어난 후각을 가지고 있어요. 나비는 혀가 없어요. 그러면 어떻게 맛을 느낄까요? 나비는 발로 맛을 느낀답니다. 나비의 미각은 나비의 뛰어난 감각 중 하나예요. 나비는 귀가 없어요. 그러면 어떻게 소리를 들을까요? 나비는 날개에 달린 털로 소리를 느껴요. 나비는 뛰어난 청각을 지니고 있지요.

와! 정말로 놀라운 생명체들이에요! 우리와 다르게 그들은 많은 뛰어난 감각들을 가지고 있어요.

Lesson 2

p.18

A Superhero

슈퍼히어로

안녕. 나는 개구리 펠릭스야. 나는 슈퍼히어로야. 파란 마스크와 빨간 망토를 두르고 있지.

나는 세 가지 뛰어난 감각을 가지고 있어. 나는 뛰어난 시각을 지녔어. 커다란 눈을 가지고 있어서 내 주변의 모든 것을 볼 수 있거든. 내 눈은 머리 위쪽에 달려 있어서 주변을 둘러보려고 머리를 돌릴 필요가 없다고! 나는 뛰어난 청각을 가지고 있어. 고음은 귀를 통해 들을 수 있고 저음은 피부를 통해 들을 수 있어. 나는 뛰어난 후각을 가지고 있어. 냄새로 물건을 찾을 수 있지.

나는 매우 높이 점프할 수도 있고 끈적한 혀로 물건들을 잡을 수도 있어. 이러한 것들은 뛰어난 감각들은 아니지만 내가 슈퍼히어로가 되는 데 도움을 줘.

어느 늦은 밤, 누군가가 "도와주세요!"라고 소리를 질렀어.

그 소리는 한 낡은 집에서 나오고 있었어. 집 안에는 소녀가 한 명 있었지.

"제발 도와주세요!" 그녀는 울었어. "우리 집에 모기들이 있어요. 그 모기들은 너무 작아서 내가 볼 수도 없어요. 모기들이 저를 물고 있어요."

"모기들이라고? 문제 없어! 내가 모기들을 찾을 수 있어."라고 나는 말했지.

나는 뛰어난 시각으로 주위를 둘러보았어. 소녀 말이 맞았어. 거기에는 모기들이 많이 있었어. 나는 뛰어난 후각으로 모기들의 냄새를 맡았어. 그리고 뛸 수 있는 만큼 높게 팔짝팔짝 뛰었어. 나는 끈적한 혀를 이용해서 모기들을 먹기 시작했어. 곧 모든 모기들은 사라졌어.

"오, 고마워요. 저를 도와주셨네요. 그런데 당신은 누구죠?"라고 소녀가 물었어.

"나는 펠릭스야. 나는 사람들을 도와주는 것을 좋아해."라고 내가 말했지.

"와, 당신은 진정한 슈퍼히어로예요."라고 소녀가 말했어.

•Main Idea
This story is mainly about a **superhero**.

•Identify
1. I have a super sense of sight.
2. I have a super sense of hearing.
3. I have s super sense of smell.

Comprehension Check Up

(A) 1. T   2. F   3. T
(B) 1. a   2. c   3. a
(C) **What Does Felix the Frog Have?**

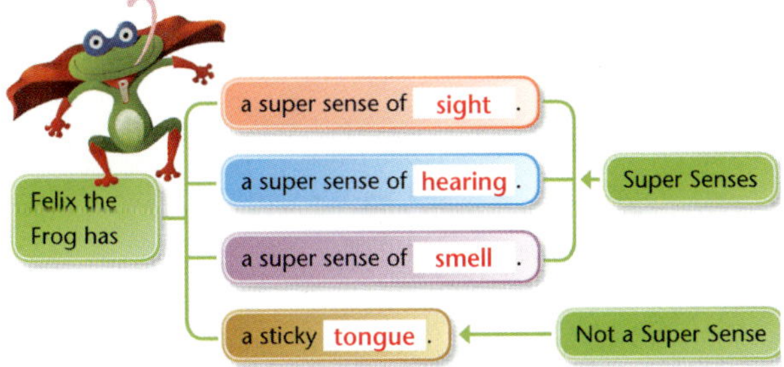

Grammar Connection

1. of smell   2. of hearing   3. of taste
4. of sight   5. of his head

On Your Own

1. hears someone yelling
2. sees the mosquitoes
3. jumps around the room

4. eats the mosquitoes

(A) 1. c   2. a   (B) 1. a   2. b

(A) 백상아리는 2개의 뛰어난 감각들을 가지고 있어요. 첫 번째로, 그것은 뛰어난 후각을 가지고 있어요. 그것은 물속에서 5 킬로미터 멀리 떨어져 있는 물고기의 냄새를 맡을 수 있어요. 다음으로, 그것은 뛰어난 청각을 가지고 있어요. 그것은 물속에서 아주 멀리 있는 소리까지 들을 수 있어요. 이 뛰어난 감각들은 백상아리가 먹이를 찾고 안전하게 지내는 데 도움이 돼요. 정말 멋진 상어지요!

(B) 개구리 펠릭스가 뛰어서 집으로 왔어요. 그는 그 소녀를 도와주어서 매우 기분이 좋았어요. 그는 사람들을 도와주는 것을 좋아해요. 그는 자신이 슈퍼히어로인 것을 좋아해요. 그는 사람들이 모기 때문에 도움이 필요하게 될 때를 정말로 좋아해요. 여러분은 그 이유를 짐작할 수 있나요?

What Does It Look Like?

그것은 어떻게 생겼나요?

Get Ready

A

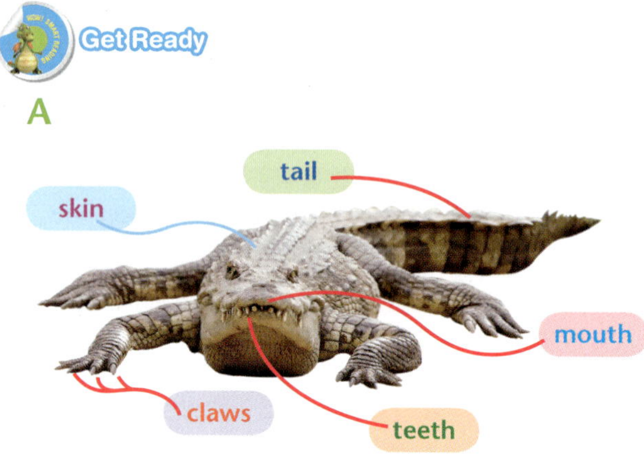

B 1. dragon   2. weighs   3. scaly
   4. reptiles   5. bite

Lesson 1

p.24

Are They Dragons?

그것들은 용인가요?

이 동물들을 봐요. 그것들은 용일까요, 아닐까요? 그것들을 자세히 살펴봐요.

이 동물은 커다란 입과 날카로운 이빨을 가지고 있어요. 고기 먹는 것을 좋아하지요. 이 동물은 건조하고 비늘로 덮인 피부에 긴 발톱을 가지고 있어요. 사냥을 할 때는 발톱을 사용하지 않아요. 큰 사냥감을 먹기 위해 입을 커다랗게 벌려요. 이것은 대부분의 시간을 물속에서 보내요. 여러분은 머리 위에 있는 이 동물의 눈이 보이나요? 이 동물은 물속에 숨어 있을 때도 먹이를 보고 사냥을 할 수 있어요. 크기가 4 미터까지 자라며 몸무게는 453 킬로그램까지 나간답니다.

이 동물을 보세요. 이 동물은 대부분의 시간을 마른 땅에서 보내요. 아주 크지만 매우 빨리 달릴 수 있지요. 이 동물은 3 미터까지 자라며 몸무게는 70 킬로그램까지 나가요. 피부는 건조하고 비늘로 덮여 있어요. 이 동물은 고기 먹기를 좋아해요. 먹이를 사냥할 때 긴 발톱을 이용해요. 이 동물이 먹이를 먹을 때는 자기 몸무게의 80 퍼센트까지 먹어치울 수 있답니다. 이 동물의 입속에는 치명적인 박테리아가 있어요. 이 말은, 이 동물이 다른 동물들을 물면 그 동물들이 아프다가 죽어버릴 수 있다는 뜻이에요.

이 동물들은 용처럼 생겼지만 진짜 용은 아니에요. 그들은 파충류예요. 파충류들은 알을 낳고, 냉혈동물이에요. 이 말은, 파충류들은 몸을 따뜻하게 유지하기 위해서 태양이 필요하다는 뜻이지요. 하나는 악어예요. 또 다른 하나는 코모도왕도마뱀이고요. 어느 것이 어느 것인지 알 수 있겠어요?

Reading Skills

- **Main Idea**
  This story is mainly about **reptiles**.

- **Compare and Contrast**
  O: When it hunts, it doesn't use its claws. It opens its mouth wide to eat large prey.
  —: It uses its long claws to hunt prey.

Comprehension Check Up

A 1. F   2. T   3. F
B 1. c   2. b   3. a
C The Komodo Dragon

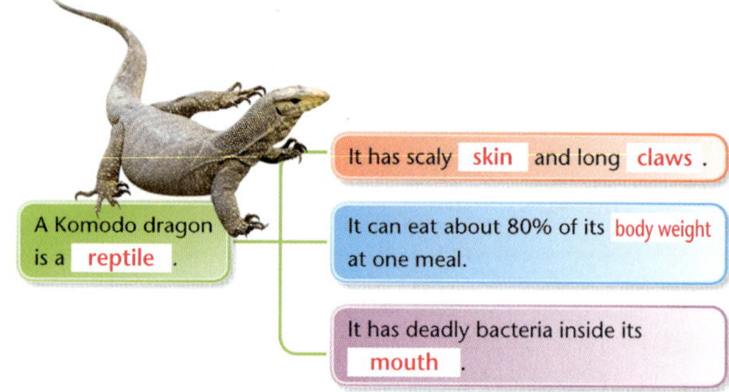

Grammar Connection

1. has   2. has   3. have
4. has   5. have

On Your Own

How Are They Alike and Different?

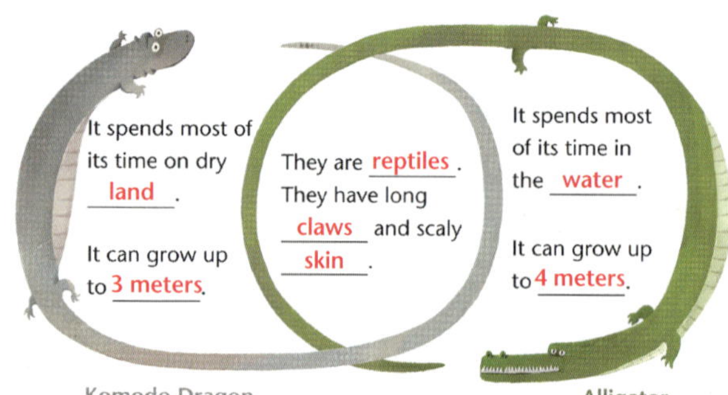

Lesson 2   p.28

Have You Ever Seen a Dragon Fly?

용이 하늘을 나는 것을 본적이 있나요?

울창한 숲 안쪽에 알 하나가 나무 아래에 있어요. 그 알은 크고 노란색이에요. 이것은 무슨 알일까요?

쉿! 알 안에서 무언가가 움직이고 있어요. 그것은 나오고 싶어해요. 알에 금이 가기 시작해요. 무언가가 알 밖으로 나오려고 발톱을 이용해요. 작은 발톱들이 갈라진 금을 밀고, 알이 열려요. 아하! 이것은 용의 알이에요.

아기 용이 알 밖으로 나와요. 아기 용은 자주색이에요. 아기 용은 발톱을 가지고 있고 피부는 비늘로 덮여 있어요. 그것은 길고 딱딱한 꼬리를 가지고 있어요. 파충류처럼 생겼지만 파충류와는 달라요. 아기 용은 두 개의 큰 날개를 가지고 있어요.

같은 시간, 대니얼이라는 이름의 소년이 그 울창한 숲 속을 걷고 있어요. 그는 이상한 소리를 들어요. 그는 바위 모퉁이 주변에서 무언가를 봐요.

"흠… 저게 뭐지? 꼬리처럼 생겼네."라고 대니얼이 말해요.

바로 그때, 아기 용이 바위 뒤에서 나와요.

"세상에! 너는 용이구나. 정말 귀엽네. 네 이름이 뭐니?"라고 대니얼이 물어요.

아기 용은 아무 말도 하지 않아요. 아기 용은 대니얼을 쳐다보기만 해요.

"음, 디오! 디오라고 이름 지어줄게. 디오, 너 날 수 있니?"라고 대니얼이 말해요.

"물론이지! 나는 나의 날개로 날 수 있어. 이리 와서 내 위에 올라 타. 내가 어디로 가면 좋겠어?"라고 디오가 말해요.

대니얼은 용 위에 올라타고 말해요. "네가 원하는 곳은 어디든 날아가. 하지만 어떤 나무에도 부딪치지 말고!"

용은 나무들 위로, 숲 위로, 그리고 구름 위까지 날아올라요. 대니얼은 활짝 웃어요.

•Main Idea
This story is mainly about a **dragon**.

•Story Elements

O: The baby dragon is purple. It has claws and scaly skin. It has a long, hard tail. It looks like a reptile but is different. The baby dragon has two big wings.

—: The dragon flies over the trees, above the forest, and up to the clouds.

A 1. F   2. T   3. F
B 1. a   2. c   3. b
C 1. a strange sound
    2. sees something
    3. comes out

1. under   2. out   3. around
4. behind

On Your Own

2. Are you a dragon?
3. Ride on me.
4. Fly high to any place.

Wrap Up   p.32

A 1. c   2. b   **B** 1. a   2. c

A 이 세상에는 많은 종류의 파충류들이 있어요. 악어, 뱀, 도마뱀, 그리고 거북이들이 파충류에 속해요. 파충류들은 몸에 비늘로 덮인 건조한 피부를 가지고 있어요. 그들은 냉혈동물이에요. 그래서 누워서 햇살을 쬐며 몸을 따뜻하게 해줘요.

B 대니얼과 디오는 하늘 높이 날고 있어요. 바람이 대니얼의 머리카락을 날리고 있어요. 그들은 파란 하늘과 하얀 구름, 그리고 초록색 나무 꼭대기들을 봐요. 그들은 저 멀리 아래에 있는 코모도왕도마뱀을 내려다봐요. 코모도왕도마뱀은 부러워하는 얼굴로 그들을 쳐다봐요. 왜냐하면 코모도왕도마뱀은 날 수가 없기 때문이에요.

Different Looks

다른 생김새

A

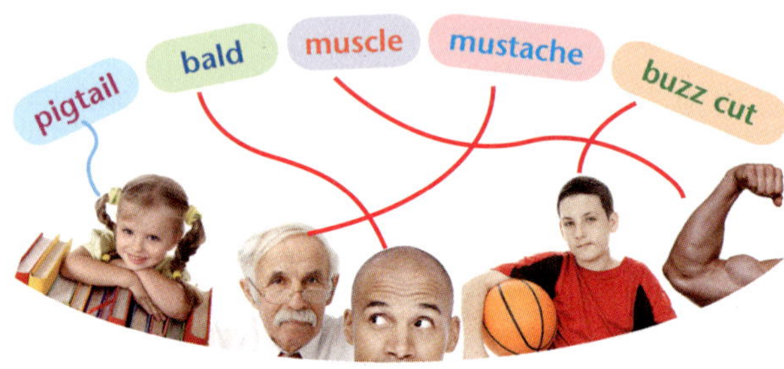

B
1. dimples
2. scratchy
3. dye
4. hairstylist
5. screams

Reading Skills

- **Main Idea**
  This story is mainly about different looks.

- **Description**
  ○: He has light skin. His eyes are big and blue. His hair is short and blond. He has a wide forehead and thin lips.
  —: He has a buzz cut. He is strong and has a lot of muscles on his body. His shoulders are very big. He is neither tall nor short. He also has a charming smile.

Comprehension Check Up

(A) 1. F   2. F   3. T
(B) 1. b   2. c   3. b
(C) 1. light   2. dimples   3. mustache
     4. muscles

Grammar Connection

1. eyes   2. hair
3. principal, school   4. wrinkles, forehead
5. muscles, body

On Your Own

What Do They Look Like?

Lesson 1

How Do They Look?

그들은 어떻게 생겼나요?

사람들은 다른 생김새를 가지고 있어요. 여러분 주위의 사람들을 보세요. 그들은 어떻게 생겼나요? 다른 사람들을 좀 더 가까이 살펴봐요.

마크를 봐요. 그는 밝은색 피부를 갖고 있어요. 그의 눈은 크고 파란색이에요. 그의 머리는 짧은 금발이에요. 그는 넓은 이마와 얇은 입술을 가지고 있어요. 그는 물감으로 그림 그리기를 정말로 좋아해서 지저분해요.

제니를 봐요. 그녀는 마크의 친한 친구예요. 그녀의 피부는 어둡지도 밝지도 않아요. 그녀의 눈은 갈색이고 작아요. 제니의 머리는 긴 생머리예요. 그리고 그녀는 땋은 머리를 하고 있어요. 그녀는 웃을 때 보조개가 있어요.

존을 봐요. 그는 마크가 다니는 학교의 교장 선생님이에요. 그는 키가 작고 대머리예요. 그는 따가워 보이는 가는 콧수염을 갖고 있어요. 그의 이마에는 주름살이 있고 항상 안경 너머로 학생들을 쳐다봐요.

마이클을 봐요. 그는 마크의 체육 선생님이에요. 그는 아주 짧게 깎은 머리를 하고 있어요. 그는 힘이 세고 몸에는 근육이 많아요. 그의 어깨는 아주 넓어요. 그는 키가 크지도 작지도 않아요. 그는 또한 매력적인 미소를 가지고 있어요.

여러분 주변의 모든 사람은 다르게 생겼을 수 있지만 멋져 보일 수도 있어요. 여러분이 알고 있는 사람들을 생각해봐요. 그들은 어떻게 생겼나요? 여러분은 어떤가요? 여러분은 어떻게 생겼나요? 거울을 볼 때 스스로에게 물어보세요. 나는 어떻게 생겼지?

Who Is Who?

누가 누구지?

레지와 셜리는 남매예요. 그들은 쌍둥이라서 같아보여요. 둘 다 밝은색 피부와 커다랗고 파란 눈을 가지고 있어요. 둘 모두 윤기 나는 갈색 머리카락을 가지고 있어요. 그리고 두 사람 다 아주 밝은 미소를 가지고 있어요. 심지어 목소리도 닮아서 사람들은 누가 누구인지 구분하지 못할 정도랍니다.

오늘, 레지와 셜리는 미용실에 가고 있어요. 그들은 새로운 헤어스타일을 원해요. 레지는 짧은 머리가 멋지다고 생각해서 스포츠 머리를 원해요. 또한 그는 그의 머리를 빨간색으로 염색하고 싶어해요. 빨간색은 그가 가장 좋아하는 색이에요. 셜리는 곱슬머리가 좋다고 생각해서 퍼머를 하기를 원해요. 그녀는 그녀가 가장 좋아하는 가수처럼 머리가 곱슬거리기를 원해요. 레지와 셜리는 그들의 새로운 헤어스타일에 흥분이 돼요.

미용실에서 레지와 셜리는 헤어 디자이너인 조앤을 만나요. 레지는 조앤에게 짧은 빨간색 머리를 원한다고 얘기해요. 셜리는 조앤에게 곱슬머리를 원한다고 말해요.

조앤이 "아무 문제 없어. 이리 와서 앉아라."라고 말해요.

조앤은 그들이 더럽혀지지 않도록 커다란 가운들을 레지와 셜리에게 둘러줘요. 의자에 앉아 있는 동안 레지와 셜리는 졸음이 와요. 곧 그들은 깊이 잠들어요.

조앤은 그들의 머리를 자르기 시작해요. 윙, 윙, 윙. 싹둑, 싹둑, 싹둑. 그녀는 쌍둥이들의 머리를 손질해요. 얼마 후에, 그녀는 손질을 마쳐요.

"오케이. 끝났어요. 얘들아, 눈을 떠 보렴."이라고 조앤이 말해요.

"으아아아아악!" 셜리가 비명을 질러요.

"아아아안돼애애!" 레지가 비명을 질러요.

"뭐가 문제지?" 조앤이 물어요. "헤어스타일이 마음에 들지 않니?"

레지와 셜리의 가운을 벗기면서 그녀는 뭐가 문제인지 알았어요. 그녀는 실수를 했어요. 그녀는 그들의 헤어스타일을 뒤바꿔버렸어요. 조앤이 레지를 봐요. 그는 아름다운 곱슬머리를 하고 있어요. 조앤이 셜리를 봐요. 그녀는 아름다운 빨간색 스포츠 머리를 하고 있어요.

"어, 안돼!" 조앤이 말해요.

Reading Skills

- **Main Idea**
  This story is mainly about **twins** who change their hairstyles.

- **Compare and Contrast**
  ○: Reg thinks short hair looks good, so he wants a buzz cut. Also, he wants to dye his hair red.
  —: Shirley thinks curly hair looks good, so she wants a perm. She wants her hair to be curly, just like her favorite singer.

Comprehension Check Up

Ⓐ 1. T   2. F   3. F
Ⓑ 1. c   2. b   3. c
Ⓒ 1. twins   2. hair salon   3. large gowns
   4. mistake

Grammar Connection

1. wants   2. looks   3. thinks
4. takes   5. sees

On Your Own

What Hairstyles Do They Want?

Wrap Up
p.42

Ⓐ 1. b   2. c   Ⓑ 1. a   2. b

Ⓐ 제이크는 많은 음식들을 먹었어요. 그가 가장 좋아하는 음식은 기름에 튀긴 닭과 햄버거예요. 그래서 그는 그것들을 줄곧 먹었어요. 제이크는 너무 살이 많이 쪘어요. 그것은 그를 슬프게 했어요. 그는 더 날씬해지고 싶었어요. 그는 매일 운동을 하고 식단을 바꿨어요. 이제 그는 달라 보여요. 그는 호리호리하고, 더 많은 근육이 있어요. 여러분도 그처럼 여러분의 외모를 바꾸고 싶나요?

Ⓑ 집에 오는 길에, 레지와 셜리는 자신들의 헤어스타일을 좀 더 자세히 보았어요. "얘, 레지. 나는 빨간색 머리가 맘에 들어."라고 셜리가 말해요. "내 빨간색 원피스와 잘 어울리는 것 같아." "그래, 네 말이 맞아. 그리고 나는 내 곱슬머리가 좋아. 매일 아침마다 머리를 빗을 필요가 없잖아."라고 레지가 말해요. "그런데 딱 한 가지 문제가 있어." 셜리가 말해요. "엄마에게 우리의 새 머리를 보여줘야만 하잖아." "아, 안돼!" 레지와 셜리가 말해요.

Helpful Plants
도움이 되는 식물들

Get Ready

A

cotton hike fever medicine walking stick

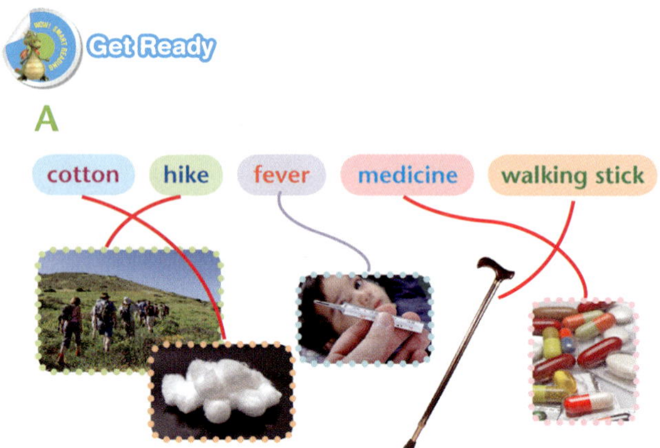

B
1. stuffed   2. campfire   3. stomachache
4. helpful   5. hurt

Lesson 1
p.44

How Do Plants Help You?

식물들은 여러분을 어떻게 도와 줄까요?

식물들은 여러 가지 방법으로 여러분을 도와줘요. 식물들은 여러분을 어떻게 도와줄까요?

여러분은 매일 음식을 먹어요. 식물들은 여러분에게 먹을 음식을 제공해줘요. 수박, 감자, 당근은 식물에서 나오지요. 여러분은 옷을 입어요. 여러분이 입고 있는 옷을 살펴보세요. 목화로 만들어졌나요? 어떤 옷들은 목화로 만들어져요. 목화도 식물에서 나오지요. 종이, 티슈, 그리고 장난감은 목재로 만들어져요. 목재도 나무에서 나지요. 어떤 식물들은 약으로 사용돼요. 여러분이 아플 때 어떤 식물들은 여러분의 기분을 더 낮게 만들어 줄 수 있어요. 코가 막혔을 때는 박하를 사용해봐요. 그것은 코가 뚫리는 데 도움을 준답니다.

알로에 베라는 매우 도움이 되는 식물이에요. 이것은 초록색이고 즙이 많답니다. 사람들은 알로에 베라로 도움이 되는 것들을 만들어요. 피부에 상처가 났을 때 알로에 젤을 발라봐요. 알로에 젤은 피부를 치료하는 데 도움이 돼요. 피부가 건조하면 알로에 크림을 발라봐요. 더 이상 건조하지 않을 거예요. 더러울 때는 알로에 비누로 씻어봐요. 알로에 비누는 여러분의 피부를 깨끗하게 하는 데 도움을 준답니다.

생강은 도움이 되는 또 다른 식물이에요. 생강은 뿌리예요. 만약 배가 아프다면 생강차나 생강 주스를 마셔봐요. 배가 아픈 것을 가라앉히는 데 도움이 돼요. 만약 열이 난다면 생강을 조금 먹거나 마셔봐요. 열을 내리는 데 도움이 된답니다. 생강은 음식이나 사탕으로도 사용될 수 있어요.

식물들은 여러분의 생활에 유익해요. 식물은 여러분에게 음식, 옷, 약, 그리고 다른 많은 것들을 제공해줘요.

Reading Skills

- **Main Idea**
  This story tells us that plants are **helpful**.

- **Problem and Solution**
  — : If you have a stuffed nose, try some mint. / If you hurt your skin, put some aloe gel on it. / If your skin is dry, put some aloe cream on it. / If you are dirty, wash with aloe soap. / If you have a stomachache, drink some ginger in tea or juice. / If you have a fever, eat or drink some ginger.

Comprehension Check Up

A 1. T   2. F   3. F
B 1. c   2. a   3. b
C 1. tissues   2. tea   3. clothes
4. gel

Grammar Connection

1. cool   2. clear   3. clean
4. settle   5. heal

On Your Own

How Do Plants Help You?

A Girl Named Jungle Jen

정글 젠이라고 불리는 소녀

정글 젠이라는 소녀를 만나보시죠. 왜 그녀의 이름이 정글 젠인지 아나요? 그녀는 정글에서 하이킹하는 것을 좋아하거든요.

어느 날, 정글 젠이 정글을 하이킹하고 있었어요. 그녀는 커다란 바위를 보았어요. 젠은 그 큰 바위를 기어올랐어요. 하지만 떨어지고 말았어요. 그녀는 손을 다쳤어요. 손에 바를 약이 좀 필요했지요.

젠은 알로에 베라 식물을 찾아 보았어요. 알로에 베라 식물을 찾았을 때, 그녀는 알로에 젤을 손에 발랐어요. 곧, 그녀의 손은 더 이상 아프지 않았어요. 알로에 베라가 그녀의 상처를 치료했기 때문에 젠은 행복했어요.

점심시간이었어요. 정글 젠은 배가 고파서 망고나무를 찾았어요. 젠은 망고 먹는 것을 좋아해요. 곧, 그녀는 더 이상 배가 고프지 않아졌어요.

망고를 먹은 후에 정글 젠은 하루 종일 정글 속을 걸었어요. 그녀는 피곤해졌어요. 나무 막대기를 찾아보았죠. 젠은 좋은 지팡이를 찾았어요. 그녀는 더 이상 피곤함을 느끼지 않았어요.

그날 저녁, 정글 젠은 추위를 타기 시작했어요. 모닥불을 피우고 싶었죠. 그녀는 나무를 찾아보았어요. 나무를 좀 찾아 젠은 모닥불을 피웠어요. 그녀는 모닥불 옆에서 따뜻해졌고, 졸렸어요. 그녀는 자고 싶었어요. 커다란 나뭇잎을 찾아보았죠. 커다란 나뭇잎을 찾아서 그녀는 폭신한 침대를 만들었어요.

그날 밤, 정글 젠은 아주 잘 잤어요. 그녀는 정글 속에 도움이 되는 식물들이 많이 있어서 행복했어요.

Reading Skills

- **Main Character**
  The main character of this story is Jungle Jen.

- **Problem and Solution**
  —: She hurt her hand. When she found one, she put aloe gel on her hand. / Jungle Jen felt hungry, so she found a mango tree. / She felt tired. She looked for a stick. / Jungle Jen began to get cold. Jen made a campfire. / She wanted to sleep. She looked for some big leaves. When she found some, she made a soft bed.

Comprehension Check Up

Ⓐ 1. F   2. F   3. T
Ⓑ 1. c   2. c   3. c
Ⓒ 1. make a soft bed
  2. keep us warm
  3. used as medicines
  4. food to eat

Grammar Connection

1. used   2. looked   3. needed
4. decided   5. loved

On Your Own

How Did Jungle Jen Solve Her Problems in the Jungle?

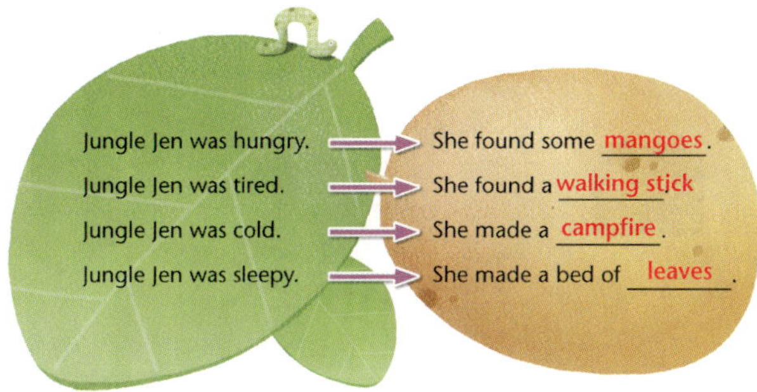

Wrap Up   p.52

Ⓐ 1. a   2. b   Ⓑ 1. c   2. b

Ⓐ 인삼은 뿌리예요. 그것은 여러분에게 여러 가지 방법으로 도움을 줄 수 있어요. 만약에 피곤하거나 아프면 인삼을 먹어봐요. 만약에 추위를 느끼면, 인삼차를 마셔봐요. 많은 사람들은 인삼을 약으로 먹거나 마셔요. 여러분도 그런가요?

Ⓑ 아침에 정글 젠은 아침 식사로 바나나를 먹었어요. 그러고 나서 집에 갔어요. 젠은 정글에 있는 식물들이 도움을 줘서 아주 행복했어요. 그녀는 다른 사람들에게 식물들이 얼마나 도움이 되는지에 대해 말하고 싶었어요. 그녀는 우리도 역시 식물들에게 도움을 주는 것이 중요하다고 말하고 싶었어요.

Unique Food from around the World
세계의 독특한 음식

5 UNIT

Get Ready

A

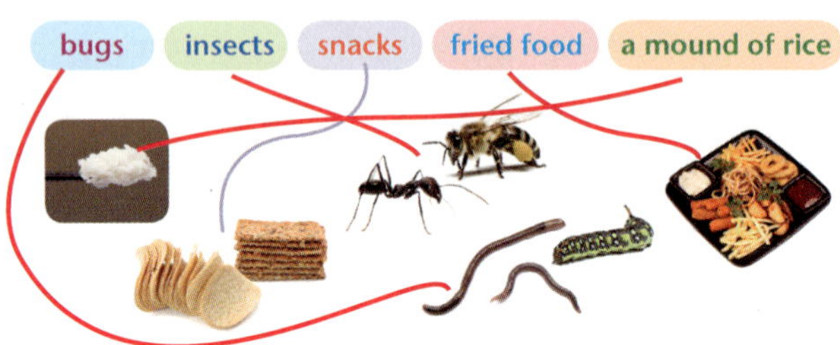

bugs　insects　snacks　fried food　a mound of rice

B　1. decorate　　2. flavor　　3. ingredients
　　4. dip　　5. crunchy

Lesson 1　　　　p.54

What Unique Food!

정말 독특한 음식들이에요!

이름: 찰리　　　　날짜: 5월 7일

방법: 전 세계 사람들이 먹는 독특한 음식에 대해서 적어보세요. 그런 다음, 그 음식들이 어떻게 요리되는지 설명해보세요.

저는 곤충으로 만들어진 세계의 독특한 음식들을 조사했습니다. 그것들은 다음과 같아요:

1. 음식 이름: 타란툴라 튀김　　국가: 캄보디아

캄보디아에서 인기 있는 요리는 튀긴 타란툴라예요. 타란툴라는 큰 거미예요. 타란툴라는 거의 어른 손바닥 크기만큼 커요. 이 음식은 아이들이 좋아하는 달콤한 간식이에요. 거미를 기름에 넣고 튀기는데 때로 그 위에 설탕을 치기도 해요. 어떨 때는 소금에 담겨지기도 하고요. 이 음식은 마치 닭고기와 포테이토칩 같은 맛이 나요.

2. 음식 이름: 바삭 메뚜기　　국가: 태국

태국에서 사람들은 바삭 메뚜기 먹는 것을 좋아해요. 메뚜기는 손가락 길이만 해요. 우선, 메뚜기를 기름에 넣고 튀겨요. 그런 다음에, 마늘과 허브를 넣어 향미를 내요. 이 음식은 바삭거리고 좋은 맛이 나요.

3. 음식 이름: 곤충 초밥　　국가: 일본

일본에서 몇몇 사람들은 특별한 초밥을 만들기 위해서 여러 종류의 곤충들을 사용해요. 그들은 바퀴벌레, 벌, 그리고 전갈과 같은 곤충들을 조심스럽게 골라요. 곤충들을 기름에 튀긴 후에 뭉쳐놓은 밥 위에 올려놓죠. 바삭한 곤충과 달콤새콤한 밥이 훌륭한 맛을 내요.

사람들은 곤충들이 건강에도 좋고 맛도 좋다고 생각해요. 사실, 곤충들은 풍부한 단백질을 가지고 있어요. 오늘날, 우리는 단백질을 얻기 위해서 많은 소와 돼지를 길러야만 해요. 하지만 곤충은 기를 필요가 없어요. 곤충들은 완벽한 음식 원재료가 될 수 있어요. 특별한 음식으로 몇몇 곤충을 사용해 보는 것은 어떨까요?

Reading Skills

•**Main Idea**
This story is mainly about unique dishes.

•**Searching for Information**
Cambodia: The spiders are fried in oil and sometimes are covered with sugar. At other times, they are dipped in salt.
Thailand: First, they fry the grasshoppers in oil. Then, garlic and herbs are added for flavor.
Japan: The insects are fried in oil, and then they are put on a mound of rice.

Comprehension Check Up

Ⓐ　1. F　　2. F　　3. T
Ⓑ　1. b　　2. b　　3. c
Ⓒ　Unique Food

Picture	Food	Country	How to Cook
	Deep _Fried_ Tarantula	Cambodia	Fry the _spiders_ in oil. Cover them with sugar or _dip_ them in salt.
	Crunchy Grasshopper	Thailand	Fry the _grasshoppers_ in oil. Add _garlic_ and herbs.
	Insect Sushi	_Japan_	Fry the _insects_ in oil. Put them on a _mound_ of rice.

Grammar Connection

1. dishes　　2. spiders　　3. grasshoppers
4. insects　　5. cows

On Your Own

Unique Food from around the World

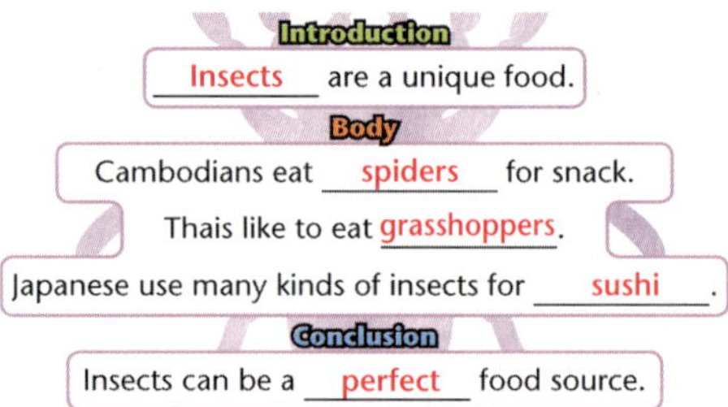

Introduction
Insects are a unique food.

Body
Cambodians eat _spiders_ for snack.
Thais like to eat _grasshoppers_.
Japanese use many kinds of insects for _sushi_.

Conclusion
Insects can be a _perfect_ food source.

Lesson 2
Lunch with Mariko

마리코와의 점심

마리코는 우리 마을에서 가장 멋진 여성이었어요. 그녀는 항상 웃는 얼굴이었어요. 어느 날, 그녀가 내 친구 토마스와 나를 점심식사에 초대했어요. 우리는 흥분됐어요. 그녀가 어떤 요리를 할지 궁금했지요.

우리는 정오에 점심식사를 하러 도착했어요.

"얘들아, 어서들 오너라. 점심 준비가 거의 다 됐어." 그녀가 말했어요.

우리는 부엌에서 나는 튀김 냄새를 맡았어요. 그 냄새는 정말로 좋았어요. 우리는 마리코가 요리하는 것을 보았어요. 우선, 마리코가 무언가를 기름에 튀겼어요. 그것들은 통통하고 갈색이었어요. 그런 다음에 그녀는 커다랗고 검은색의 무언가를 튀겼어요. 그녀는 뭉쳐놓은 밥 위에 튀김을 얹었어요. 그것들은 초밥처럼 보였어요. 마지막으로, 그녀는 노란색과 분홍색의 꽃들과 초록색 나뭇잎으로 장식을 했어요.

"자, 얘들아. 우선 이것들을 먼저 먹어봐. 만약 너희들이 좋아하면 더 만들어 줄게."라고 마리코가 말했어요.

우리 둘은 그것들을 먹어보는 것이 흥미로웠어요. "좋아, 토마스. 네가 검은색을 먹어봐. 나는 갈색을 먹을게. 준비됐어? 셋을 세면 먹는 거야. 하나, 둘, 셋."이라고 내가 말했어요.

으드득! 바삭! 우리 눌은 그것들을 먹었어요. 나는 토미스를 보았어요. 나는 그의 눈이 커지는 것을 보았어요. 그의 얼굴에 활짝 미소가 피어났어요. 그는 초밥을 좋아했어요. 그리고 나도 그것이 좋았어요.

"얘들아, 맛이 어떠니?"라고 마리코가 물었어요.

"더 주세요."라고 우리는 말했어요.

"물론이지! 음식을 더 만들기 위해 재료를 더 가지러 가자."라고 마리코가 말했어요.

우리는 마리코를 따라 밖으로 나갔어요. 그녀는 초록색 덤불로 걸어갔어요. 그녀는 큰 돌을 하나 집어 들었어요. 돌 밑에는 딱정벌레, 벌레, 그리고 거미들이 있었어요. 마리코가 그 벌레와 곤충들을 집어 들었어요. 토마스와 나는 충격을 받았어요. 그녀는 그것들로 점심을 만들었던 것이었어요. 으으으!

• **Main Idea**
This story is mainly about a special lunch.

• **Sequence**
First, Mariko fried some things in oil. / Next, she fried some large and black things. She put them on a mound of rice. / Last, she decorated them with yellow and pink flowers and green leaves.

Comprehension Check Up

Ⓐ 1. T 2. F 3. T
Ⓑ 1. b 2. a 3. a
Ⓒ 1. bushes 2. rock 3. insects

Grammar Connection

1. Mariko was a ∨ woman in our village.
2. She put it on a ∨ flower.
3. She decorated them with ∨ insects.
4. I'll eat the ∨ one.
5. She walked to some ∨ bushes.

On Your Own

1. fried / in oil 2. mound 3. decorated

Wrap Up p.62

Ⓐ 1. b 2. b Ⓑ 1. b 2. a

Ⓐ 미국에서는 핫릭스 곤충 사탕 먹는 것을 즐기는 사람들도 있어요. 핫릭스는 벌레 초콜릿이나 전갈 막대 사탕 같은 곤충 사탕을 파는 회사예요. 여러분은 바나나, 사과, 그리고 블루베리 같은 여러 가지 맛이 나는 전갈 막대 사탕들을 살 수 있어요. 먼저 여러 맛이 나는 막대 사탕을 맛있게 빨아 먹어요. 그리고 사탕을 다 먹으면, 전갈을 먹어요. 겨우 3 달러로 특별한 곤충 사탕을 먹을 수 있지요.

Ⓑ 토마스와 나는 마리고를 따라서 **부엌**으로 되돌아 갔어요. 우리는 곤충을 먹는다는 생각을 좋아하진 않았지만 그 맛은 정말 좋았어요.

"얘들아, 그래서 이번에는 무엇을 먹겠니?" 마리코가 물었어요.

"딱정벌레 찾으셨어요?" 토마스가 물었어요. "전 딱정벌레를 먹어보고 싶거든요."

"그리고 저는 벌레를 먹어보고 싶어요." 내가 말했어요.

"하지만 이번에는 꽃은 넣지 말아주세요. 그냥 벌레만 주세요." 나는 말했어요.

"그냥 벌레만 달라고?" 마리코가 물었어요. "으으으!"

An Amazing Story
놀라운 이야기

Get Ready

A

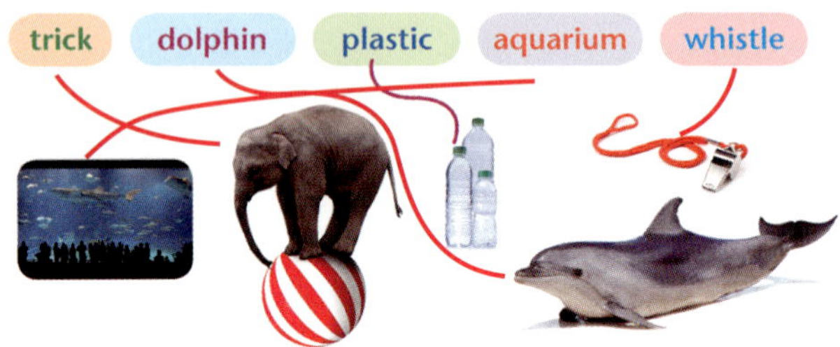

B
1. amazing   2. swallows   3. smart
4. remove   5. save

Lesson 1   p.64

Lucky Dolphins

운이 좋은 돌고래들

정말 놀라운 이야기를 듣고 싶나요?

이 이야기는 중국의 푸순 마을에서 시작됐어요. 돌고래 두 마리가 수족관에서 수영을 하고 있었어요. 수영장에는 플라스틱이 있었는데, 돌고래들이 이 플라스틱을 좀 삼켰어요. 하지만 돌고래들은 플라스틱을 소화할 수 없었어요. 이 플라스틱이 돌고래의 위장을 아프게 했지요. 얼마 후, 돌고래들은 먹이를 먹지 않았어요. 조련사들은 걱정을 했어요. 조련사들은 돌고래들의 위장에서 플라스틱을 빼내려고 시도를 했어요. 하지만 실패했죠. 돌고래들은 매우 약해졌어요. 만약에 플라스틱을 빼내지 못한다면 돌고래들이 죽을 수도 있었어요.

조련사들 중 한 명이 아이디어를 냈어요. 그는 세계에서 가장 키가 큰 사람인 바오시순을 기억해냈어요. 그는 2 미터 36 센티미터의 키에 팔 길이가 1 미터 6 센치미터였어요. 조련사는 바오가 돌고래들을 구할 수 있을 거라고 생각했어요. 그는 그의 긴 팔로 돌고래의 위장까지 닿을 수 있을 거예요. 그러면, 그는 플라스틱을 꺼낼 수도 있을 거예요. 조련사는 바오에게 전화를 했고, 바오는 돌고래들을 구하는 일을 도와주는 데 동의했어요. 조련사들이 돌고래의 입을 벌렸어요. 그런 다음에 수건으로 돌고래의 이빨을 감쌌어요. 이제 돌고래의 이빨은 바오를 다치게 하지는 못할 거였죠. 그의 긴 팔로 바오는 돌고래의 위장 속에 닿았어요. 그는 플라스틱을 빼냈어요. 바오가 돌고래들을 구했어요.

이제, 돌고래들은 다시 행복해요. 많은 사람들이 수족관에 있는 돌고래들을 보러 와요. 이 모든 것이 세상에서 가장 키가 큰 사람 덕분이지요. 정말 놀라운 이야기이지요!

Reading Skills

• Main Idea
This story is mainly about saving the dolphins.

• Problem and Solution
○: There was plastic in the pool, and they swallowed some. But the dolphins couldn't digest the plastic. The plastic hurt their stomachs. Soon, they stopped eating their food.

—: With his long arms, Bao reached inside the dolphins' stomachs. He took out the plastic. Bao saved the dolphins.

Comprehension Check Up

Ⓐ 1. T   2. T   3. F
Ⓑ 1. a   2. b   3. b
Ⓒ Dolphins' Lucky Day

Problem
The dolphins swallowed the ___plastic___.

Solution
Bao ___removed___ the plastic from the dolphins' stomachs.

Problem
The dolphins' ___teeth___ could hurt Bao.

Solution
The workers wrapped ___towels___ around the dolphins' teeth.

Grammar Connection

1. Two dolphins / were swimming in an aquarium.
2. The plastic / hurt their stomachs.
3. The workers / were worried.
4. Then, he / could take out the plastic.
5. The dolphins' teeth / couldn't hurt Bao.

On Your Own

1. swallowed   2. digest   3. hurt
4. eating   5. weak

Those Amazing Dolphins!

저 놀라운 돌고래들!

여러분, 안녕하세요. 제 이름은 데이브예요. 저는 이 수족관의 돌고래 조련사입니다. 저의 돌고래들은 매우 영리하답니다. 저는 그들을 제 호각으로 훈련시켰어요. 그들이 제 호각 소리를 들으면 재주를 부린답니다. 보세요. 호르륵! 돌고래들이 제 옆쪽으로 오지요. 호르륵, 호르륵! 돌고래들이 여러분들에게 지느러미를 흔드네요. 모두들 저의 사랑스러운 돌고래들에게 인사해주세요.

저는 또한 저의 돌고래들이 읽을 수 있도록 훈련시켰어요. 제가 이 카드를 돌고래들에게 보여 줄 거예요. 나의 사랑스러운 돌고래들아, 이 카드에 있는 단어들을 읽어보렴.

> 공중으로 높게 점프한 후 뒤로 공중돌기를 해라.

이제, 나에게 묘기를 보여 주렴. 돌고래들이 번갯불처럼 헤엄치는 걸 보세요. 그들이 공중으로 어떻게 높이 점프한 후 뒤로 공중돌기를 하는지 보세요.

모두들 쇼를 즐기고 계시나요? 이번에는 제가 호각을 불지 않을 거예요. 쉿! 여러분. 이번 묘기가 돌고래들의 최고의 묘기가 될 거예요. 지원자가 필요해요. 거기! 빨간 셔츠를 입고 있는 소년. 어때요? 이 카드 위에 몇 가지 묘기를 적을 수 있겠어요? 고마워요! 쉬잇~! 이번에는 이 카드를 돌고래들에게 보여주지 않을 거예요. 돌고래들아, 카드에 적혀있는 묘기를 우리에게 보여줘. 보세요! 돌고래들이 두 개의 링을 점프해서 통과하네요. 잠깐만. 돌고래들이 어디로 가는 거지요? 돌고래들이 저에게 곧바로 오네요. 돌고래들이 공중으로 점프를 하네요… 첨벙! 세상에! 돌고래들이 저를 완전히 물에 젖게 만드네요. 카드를 볼까요.

> 두 개의 링을 통과해라. 그리고 나서 데이브를 완전히 물에 젖게 만들어라.

보세요! 돌고래들이 카드를 읽지도 않고 묘기를 부렸어요. 오, 정말로 놀라운 돌고래들이에요!

Reading Skills

- **Main Idea**
  This story is mainly about training dolphins.

- **Sequence**
  —: The dolphins come to my side. / They wave their flippers at you. / Look how they jump high in the air and do a backflip. / They jump through two hoops. / They soak me with water.

Comprehension Check Up

A. 1. T   2. T   3. F
B. 1. c   2. b   3. c
C. 1. side   2. flippers   3. backflip
   4. hoops

Grammar Connection

1. trainers / work   2. man / trained
3. dolphins / swim   4. They / jump
5. crowd / cheers

On Your Own

Why Are the Dolphins Amazing ?

Wrap Up   p.72

A. 1. b   2. c   B. 1. b   2. a

A. 여러분은 바오가 돌고래들을 구한 최초의 키 큰 사람이 아니라는 사실을 믿나요? 1978년에 미국의 농구선수인 클리포드 레이는 캘리포니아 수족관에 있는 돌고래를 구해 주었어요. 그 돌고래는 금속 조각을 삼켜서 죽을 위험에 처해 있었어요. 클리포드는 그의 1 미터 14 센티미터나 되는 긴 팔로 그 돌고래의 위장에서 그 금속 조각을 꺼내었어요. 그가 그 돌고래를 구했답니다.

B. 쇼를 마친 후에 데이브는 돌고래들에게 먹이를 줘요. 그들은 먹이를 받아먹는 것을 좋아해요. 그것이 데이브가 그들을 훈련시키는 방법이에요. 그 돌고래들은 재주를 부릴 것이고, 그래서 먹이를 받아먹을 수 있어요. 그가 호각을 불면 그들은 먹이를 한 개 받아먹을 거라는 것을 알고 있어요. 그들이 카드를 읽으면, 그들은 4개의 먹이들을 받아먹을 거라는 것도 알고 있지요. 여러분은 그들의 먹이가 무엇인지 짐작할 수 있나요? 물론 물고기지요!

Beyond Words
말을 넘어서

7 UNIT

Get Ready

A

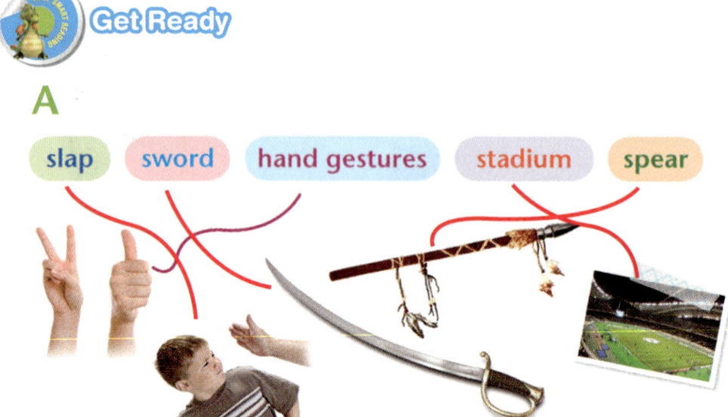

slap sword hand gestures stadium spear

B
1. positive   2. gladiator   3. audience
4. celebrate   5. communicate

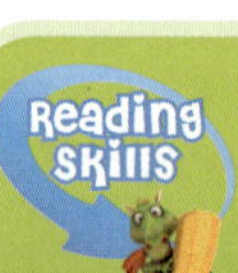

Reading Skills

- **Main Idea**
This story is mainly about **hand gestures**.

- **Describing**
— : Two boys raise their hands and head high. Then they hit their palms together. They might say, "High-five." / A cute girl shows thumbs up. She closes her fists with her thumbs upward. / The scuba diver in the water gives the okay sign by making a circle with two fingers.

Lesson 1
p.74

Hand Gestures

손동작들

가끔 여러분은 하이 파이브나 오케이 사인과 같은 손동작을 사용해요. 여러분은 언제 손동작을 사용하나요? 왜 그런 손동작을 사용하나요? 그런 손동작의 의미는 무엇이고, 어디에서 왔을까요?

두 명의 소년들이 그들의 손을 올리고 높이 위로 향하고 있어요. 그러고 나서 그들의 손바닥을 서로 부딪쳐요. 그들은 아마도 "하이 파이브"라고 말할 거예요. 이 동작의 이름은 손의 다섯 손가락과 손을 높게 올리고 있는 것에서 왔어요. 첫 번째 하이 파이브는 1977년 미국 야구장에서 행해졌어요. 로스앤젤레스 야구 선수가 홈런을 쳤을 때, 다른 선수가 축하해 주려고 그 선수의 손을 찰싹 때리기 위해 손을 들었어요. 지금은 사람들이 어떤 일을 축하하려고 이 손동작을 사용해요.

귀여운 소녀가 엄지손가락들을 세워요. 그녀는 엄지손가락을 올린 채 두 주먹을 쥐어요. 엄지손가락을 세우는 것은 '잘했어요' 또는 '수고했어요'라는 의미이고, 긍정적인 신호예요. 이 동작은 고대 로마시대 콜로세움의 관중들에게서 나왔어요. 관중들은 싸움에서 진 검투사의 생사에 대해 투표를 했어요. 엄지손가락을 세우면 살려주고, 엄지손가락을 내리면 죽이라는 표시였어요.

물속에서 스쿠버 다이버들은 두 손가락으로 동그라미를 만들어 OK 사인을 해요. 여러분이 음식을 먹을 때 음식을 입에 넣은 채로 말하는 것은 예의 바르지 못한 행동이에요. 이럴 때는, '아주 맛있다' 또는 '괜찮다'를 의미하는 OK 사인을 사용할 수 있어요.
손동작은 의사소통에 좋은 수단이에요. 손동작은 여러분이 말하는 단어들보다 더 많은 것을 의미할 수도 있어요. 여러분이 가끔 사용하는 다른 동작들을 생각해보세요. 여러분은 그것들이 무엇을 의미한다고 생각하나요? 그러한 손동작은 어디서 왔나요?

Comprehension Check Up

A 1. T   2. F   3. F
B 1. c   2. c   3. b
C When Do People Use Hand Gestures?

They use this to **celebrate** something.

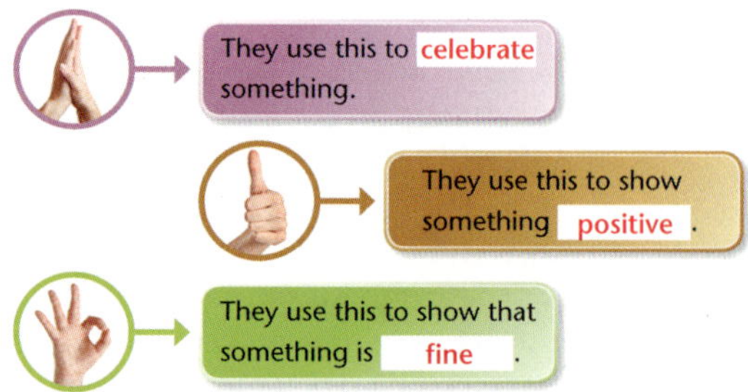

They use this to show something **positive**.

They use this to show that something is **fine**.

Grammar Connection

1. When   2. Why   3. How
4. Where   5. What

On Your Own

Which Hand Gestures Do You Prefer?

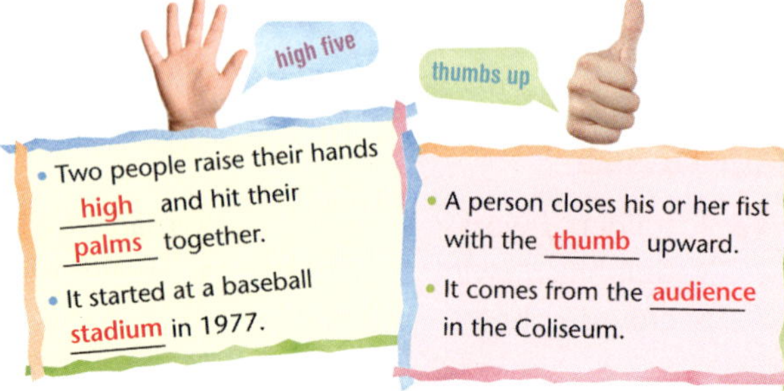

- Two people raise their hands **high** and hit their **palms** together.
- It started at a baseball **stadium** in 1977.

- A person closes his or her fist with the **thumb** upward.
- It comes from the **audience** in the Coliseum.

A Day at the Coliseum

콜로세움의 어느 날

"이 봐, 마르쿠스." 나는 소리를 질러요. "서둘러. 그렇지 않으면 우리는 대결을 볼 수 없을 거야."

나의 가장 친한 친구인 마르쿠스와 나는 콜로세움으로 가고 있어요. 우리는 검투사의 싸움을 볼 예정이에요. 나는 늦고 싶지 않아요. 사람들이 너무 많아서 우리는 군중들 속에서 밀면서 가야 해요. 거기에는 로마 병사들도 있어요. 그들은 서로에게 경례를 하고 있어요.

마침내 우리는 도착해요. 우리는 검투사들을 내려다 봐요. 그들은 정말로 커요. 그리고 굉장히 강해 보여요.

"세상에, 안토니." 마르쿠스가 말해요. "저쪽에 있는 스파르타쿠스를 봐. 그는 커다란 금색 헬멧을 머리에 쓰고 있어. 손에는 날카로운 검을 들고 있네. 나는 그가 이겼으면 좋겠어."

"절대로 안 돼." 내가 마르쿠스에게 말해요. "나는 막시무스가 좋아. 그는 은색 마스크를 얼굴에 쓰고 있어. 손에는 긴 창을 들고 있어. 나는 그가 이겼으면 좋겠어."

싸움이 시작돼요. 두 명의 검투사들은 잘 싸워요. 군중들은 환호하고 있어요. 관중들은 검투사들의 싸움을 즐기고 있어요. 마르쿠스와 나도 싸움을 즐겨요. 얼마 후, 싸움이 끝나요. 황금 헬멧을 쓰고 있는 스파르타쿠스가 굉장히 잘 싸웠어요. 그가 싸움에서 이겼어요. 이제 두 명의 검투사들이 콜로세움의 가운데에 서 있어요. 그들은 막시무스를 살릴지 죽일지에 대해 관중들이 결정을 내리기를 기다리고 있어요.

갑자기, 모든 관중들이 함성을 지르기 시작해요. 마르쿠스와 나도 함성을 질러요. 그리고, 우리 모두 엄지손가락을 올리는 동장을 취해요. 막시무스는 잘 싸웠어요. 우리는 막시무스가 살기를 원해요.

집으로 오는 길에 마르쿠스와 나는 행복해요. 콜로세움에서의 아주 멋진 하루였어요! 스파르타쿠스와 막시무스는 둘 다 굉장한 검투사예요. 나는 다음 번에는 누가 이길지 궁금해요.

Reading Skills

- **Main Idea**
  This story is mainly about the fighting in the **Coliseum**.

- **Details**
  —: He has a large golden helmet on his head. In his hand, he has a sharp sword. / He has a silver mask on his face. In his hand, he has a long spear.

Comprehension Check Up

Ⓐ 1. T   2. F   3. T
Ⓑ 1. c   2. a   3. b

Ⓒ **Roman Gladiators**

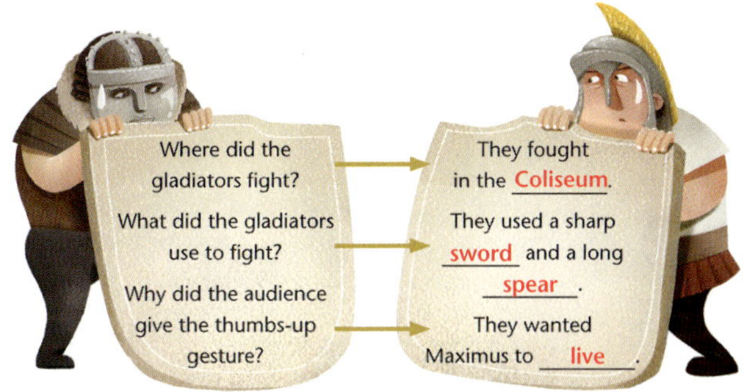

Grammar Connection

1. are going   2. is watching   3. are saluting
4. is cheering   5. are enjoying

On Your Own

1. gladiators   2. both   3. wins
4. thumbs-up

Wrap Up   p.82

Ⓐ 1. b   2. c   Ⓑ 1. c   2. a

Ⓐ 여자 아이가 V자를 그려요. 그녀는 손으로 주먹을 만들어요. 그리고 나서 그녀는 가운데와 둘째 손가락을 세워서 서로 떨어지게 해요. V자를 그리는 손동작에는 다른 의미들이 있어요. 이 손동작은 승리와 평화를 의미해요. 그것은 또한 사람들이 사진을 찍을 때 사용하기도 해요. 여러분도 이 손동작을 사용하나요?

Ⓑ 집에서 마르쿠스와 나는 우리가 검투사들인 것처럼 행동해요. 우리의 칼은 서로 쾅 부딪치고, 우리는 집 주변을 뛰어다녀요. 마침내 싸움이 끝났어요, 우리는 마치 관중들의 함성을 듣는 것처럼 행동해요. 그리고 나서 관중들이 엄지손가락을 올리자, 우리는 공중으로 높이 뛰어올라요. 우리는 서로 하이파이브를 하고 소리를 질러요. "만세."

Science inside Balls

공 안의 과학

p.83

8 UNIT

 **Get Ready**

A

B
1. direction   2. surface   3. bounces
4. teammates   5. grips

Lesson 1   p.84

Missing Balls

잃어버린 공들

안녕, 모두들.

나는 공 4개가 들어있는 가방을 잃어버렸어. 내 공들을 본 적이 있니? 만약 그 공들을 본다면 내게 가져다 줘. 그것들은 내 공들이야.

내 농구공은 크고 오렌지색이야. 네가 이 공을 잡으면, 오돌토돌한 것을 느낄 거야. 내 야구공은 작고 딱딱하고 흰색이야. 이 공을 던질 때, 공에 있는 바늘땀들을 느낄 수 있을 거야. 내 테니스 공은 작고 부드럽고 노란색이야. 네가 이 공을 잡으면, 느낌이 보송보송할 거야. 마지막으로 내 축구공은 크고 둥근 모양이야. 네가 내 축구공을 차면, 딱딱한 느낌이 들거야.

나는 내 공들을 정말로 좋아해. 제발 내 공들을 찾아줘.

고마워.

스티븐으로부터

안녕, 스티븐,

내가 네 가방을 운동장에서 찾았어. 하지만 나는 네 공들에 대해서 궁금해. 아래 빈 공간에 내 질문에 대해서 대답해 줄 수 있니?

질문 1: 너의 농구공 표면에는 작은 돌기들이 있구나. 왜 그런 거니?

→ 작은 돌기들은 그 공을 잘 잡도록 도와줘. 농구 선수들은 손으로 그 공을 잡아서 골대로 집어넣거든.

질문 2: 너의 야구공에는 빨간 실밥이 있구나. 왜 그런 거니?

→ 야구공에 있는 실밥은 공중에서 곡선으로 가거나 방향을 바꾸는 데 도움을 줘. 투수들은 자기가 원하는 곳으로 야구공을 던질 수 있지.

질문 3: 너의 테니스공의 표면은 보송보송하구나. 왜 그런 거니?

→ 테니스공의 보송보송한 털은 공이 라켓에서 튀는 데 도움을 줘. 테니스 선수들은 라켓으로 공을 잘 튀기거나 회전시킬 수 있지.

만약에 빈 공간에 답을 바르게 써 준다면, 내가 너의 공들을 분실물 센터에 놔 둘게.

러셀로부터

Reading Skills

- **Main Idea**
This story is mainly about the **reasons** that balls are different.

- **Details**
○: The small bumps help you grip the ball well. Basketball players grip it in their hand and throw it into the net. / The stitches on a baseball help it curve and change direction in the air. Pitchers can throw the baseball wherever they want. / The fuzz on a tennis ball helps the ball bounce on a racket. Tennis players can bounce and spin the ball well with a racket.

Comprehension Check Up

Ⓐ 1. T   2. T   3. F
Ⓑ 1. b   2. c   3. a

Ⓒ **Why Do Balls Look Different?**

Baseballs have _stitches_.

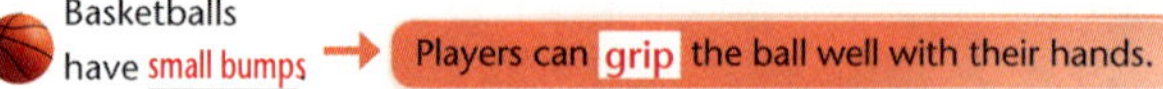
Basketballs have small bumps

Tennis balls have _fuzz_.

Grammar Connection

1. When   2. When   3. when
4. When   5. when

On Your Own

A Closer Look at Two Balls

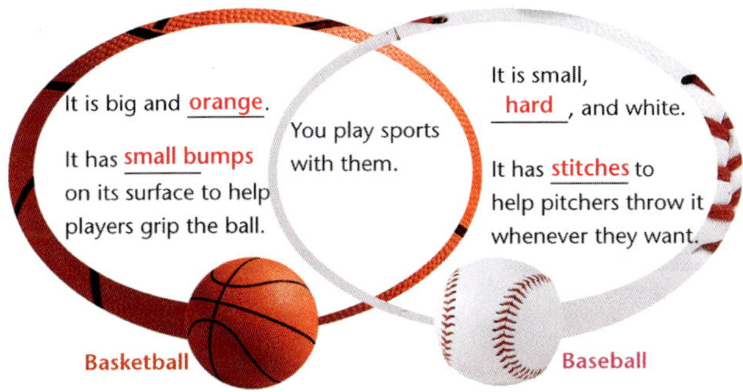

Lesson 2   p.88

Game Day

경기 날

스콧은 축구팀에서 경기를 해요. 그는 오늘의 경기를 준비하고 있어요. 첫 번째로 스콧은 그의 파란색 유니폼을 입어요. 그러고 나서, 그의 축구화를 신어요. 그런 다음에, 그는 가방을 챙겨요. 마지막으로, 그는 축구공을 챙겨요. 이런! 축구공을 찾을 수가 없어요.

스콧은 선반 위를 찾아봐요. 그의 공은 거기에 없어요. 스콧은 문 뒤쪽, 사물함 옆과 긴 의자 밑을 찾아봐요. 공은 어디에도 없어요. 스콧은 걱정되기 시작해요. 공은 어디에서 있을까요? 갑자기, 스콧은 생각이 떠올라요. 그는 자기 가방 안을 봐요. 아하! 그의 공은 거기에 있어요. 이제 그는 게임을 하러 갈 수 있어요.

축구 경기가 호각 소리와 함께 시작해요. "이봐, 이쪽으로 줘." 스콧이 소리 질러요. 그는 공을 원해요. 그의 동료가 공을 그에게 패스해줘요. 공은 공중에 높이 떴어요. 스콧은 골대 안으로 공을 튕겨 넣는 데 그의 머리를 이용해요. 골인이에요!

"야호." 스콧이 소리 질러요.

점수는 1대 0이에요. 그들은 경기에서 이길 수 있어요.

스콧이 공을 가지고 있어요. 그는 골대를 향해서 뛰어요.

"슛! 슛!" 스콧의 동료들이 소리 질러요. 하지만 골키퍼가 공을 잡을 준비가 되어있기 때문에 그는 골대를 향해 공을 차지 않아요. 스콧은 동료에게 공을 패스해요. 이제 골키퍼는 공을 잡을 수 없어요. 스콧의 동료가 공을 차서 골대에 넣어요. 이제 점수는 2대 0이에요.

"야호, 우리가 이겼다." 스콧이 소리 질러요.

경기가 끝났어요. 스콧과 그의 동료들은 경기를 이겨서 행복해요.

오늘은 정말로 멋진 날이에요.

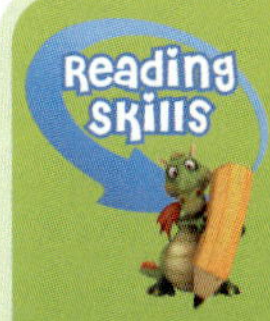

Reading Skills

- **Main Idea**
  This story is mainly about playing soccer.

- **Problem and Solution**
  - ○: He cannot find his soccer ball. / But he does not kick the ball to the net because the goalkeeper is ready to catch the ball.
  - —: He looks inside his bag. / Scott passes the ball to a teammate.

Comprehension Check Up

- (A) 1. T   2. F   3. T
- (B) 1. a   2. c   3. a
- (C) 1. puts on his uniform
  2. gets his soccer ball
  3. plays a soccer game
  4. wins the game

Grammar Connection

1. can   2. can   3. cannot
4. can   5. cannot

On Your Own

How Does Scott Solve the Problem?

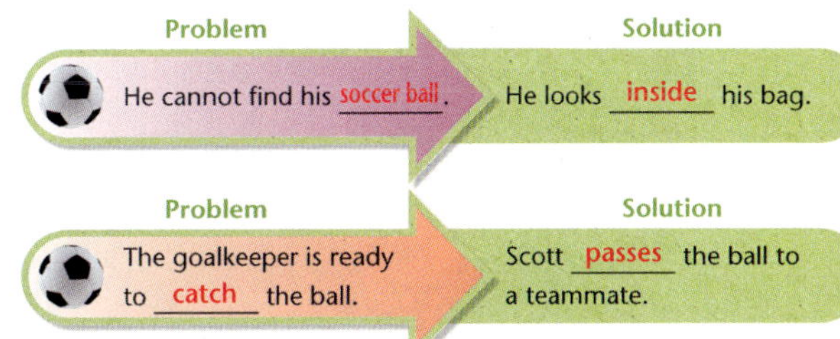

Wrap Up   p.92

- (A) 1. b   2. a
- (B) 1. a   2. b

(A) 많은 사람들은 골프 치는 것을 좋아해요. 사람들이 골프를 칠 때, 그들은 골프공을 사용해요. 골프공은 작고, 단단하고 하얀색이에요. 공 표면에는 작게 움푹 패인 구멍들이 있지요. 여러분이 골프공을 잡으면 그것은 울퉁불퉁하게 느껴져요. 여러분은 왜 골프공이 울퉁불퉁한지 그 이유를 알고 있나요? 골프 선수가 공을 치면, 작게 움푹 패인 구멍들이 공이 공중으로 멀리 날아가는 데 도움을 주기 때문이에요.

(B) 경기가 끝나고 나서 스콧과 그의 팀 동료들은 파티를 해요. 그들은 기분이 좋아요. 그들은 경기에 대해서 얘기하고 있어요.

"네가 머리를 이용해서 골을 넣은 건 최고였어." 동료가 말했어요.

"고마워." 스콧이 말했어요. "하지만 우리는 팀으로 이긴 거야. 우리가 서로 돕는다면 우리는 모든 경기를 이길 수 있을 거라고 난 확신해."

Wow! Smart Vocabulary

*전 5권 시리즈

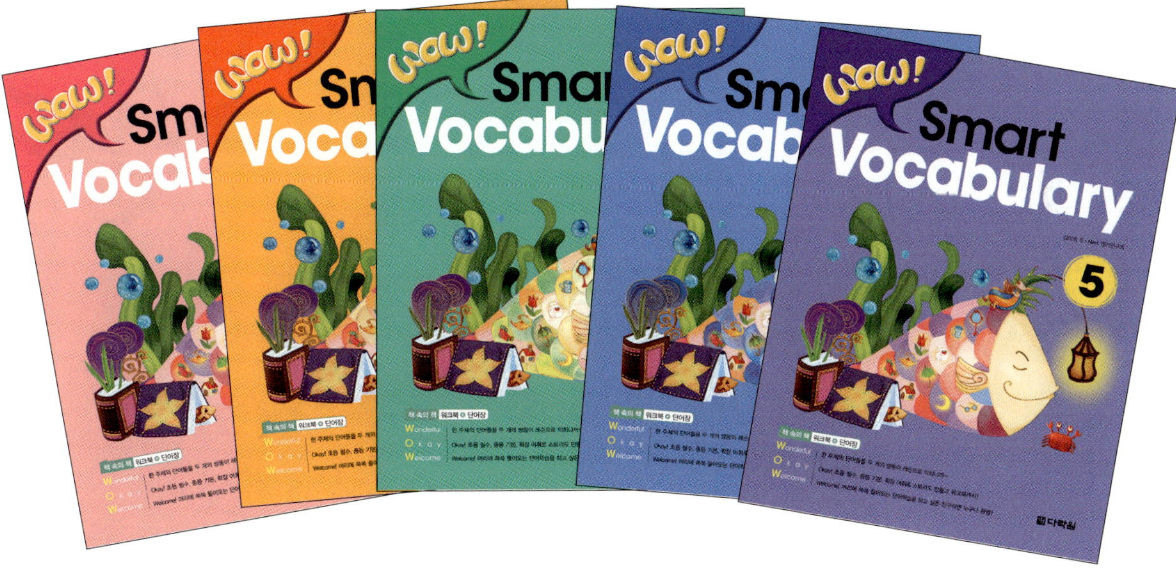

단어에서 문장을 넘어 스토리까지!

하나의 Unit을 두 개의 쌍둥이 Lesson으로 스마트하게, 입체적으로 익혀요.

- ⭐ Nonfiction과 Fiction의 **쌍둥이 Lesson으로** 하나의 주제를 **입체적으로 학습**
- ⭐ 교과부 새 기본 어휘 목록표에 따라 엄선한 **초등 · 중등 · 확장어휘 표제어 1,160개**
- ⭐ 단어에서 문장과 스토리로 나아가는 **단계적인 연습 문제**
- ⭐ 스마트한 **자기주도학습의 파트너, 워크북**
- ⭐ 책 속의 **영어문장 해석**, 표제어 및 스토리 MP3 파일 무료 다운로드,
  문제 출제 프로그램 무료 이용 www.darakwon.co.kr

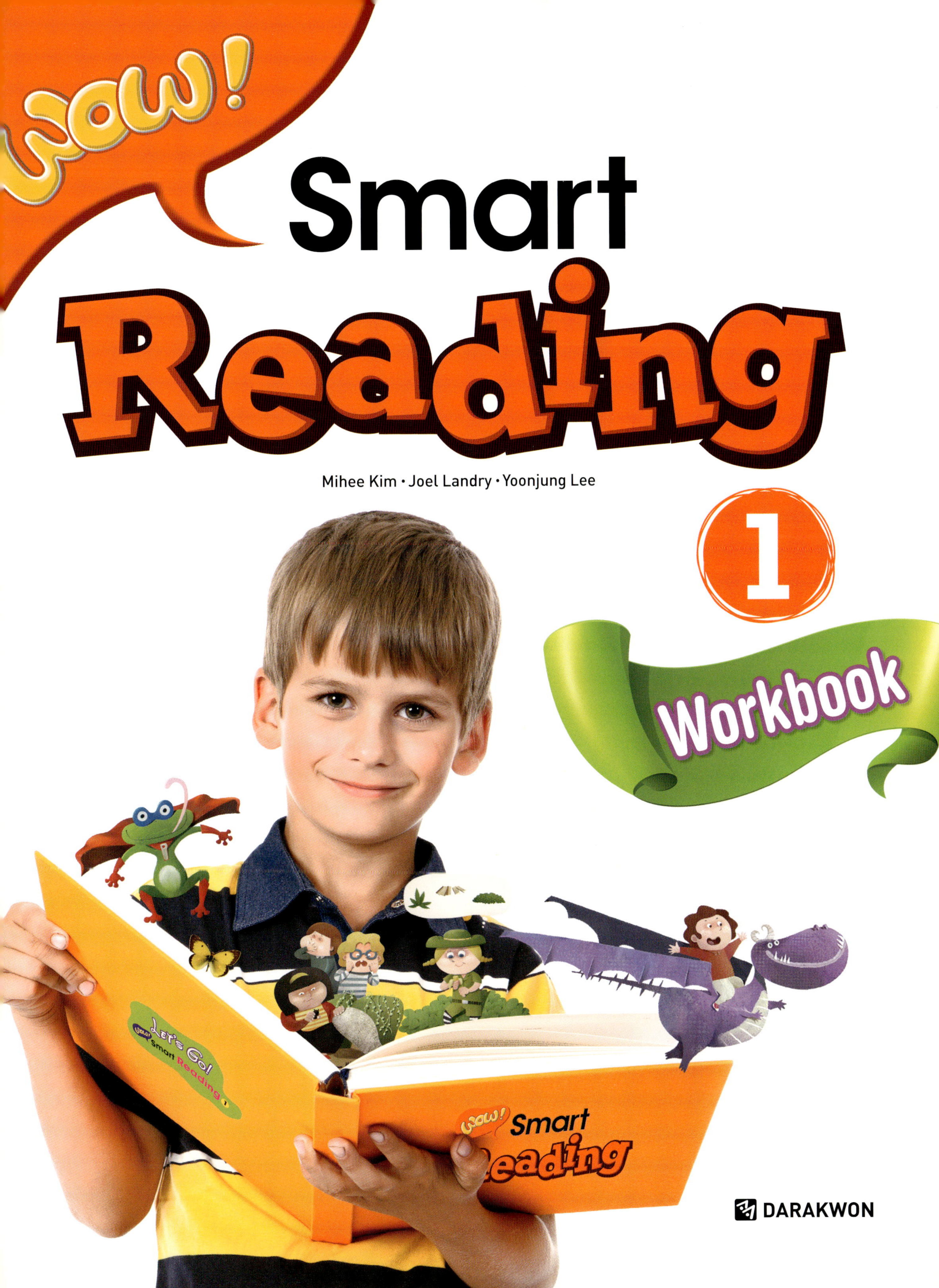

Wow!
Smart
Reading
Mihee Kim · Joel Landry · Yoonjung Lee
1
Workbook
DARAKWON

WOW! Smart Reading

1

Workbook

Contents

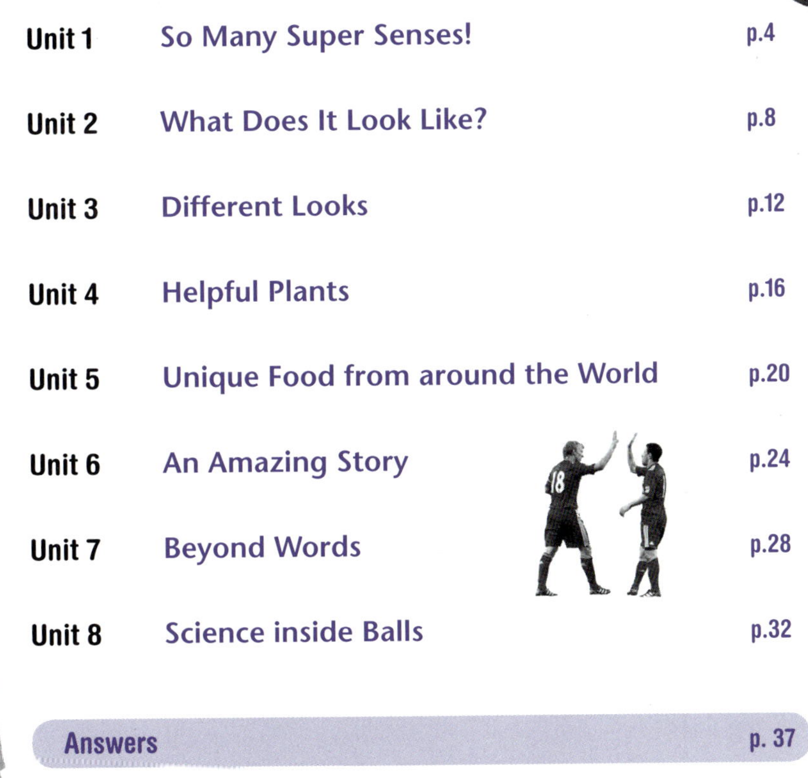

So Many Super Senses!

A Write the words and phrases in English or Korean.

1.	메기		11.	taste
2.	수염, 콧수염		12.	smell
3.	매		13.	compound eyes
4.	더듬이		14.	creature
5.	모기		15.	tongue
6.	뛰어난 감각		16.	a sense of sight
7.	끈적거리는		17.	look around
8.	초영웅, 초인		18.	through
9.	망토		19.	feel
10.	소리지르다		20.	by the way

B Complete the sentences.

1. A _________ _________ with its whole body.
   메기는 몸 전체로 맛을 느껴요.

2. It can even taste with its _________.
   그것은 심지어 수염으로도 맛을 느끼죠.

3. A _________ can see the same mouse from 1,500 meters.
   매는 똑같은 쥐를 1,500 미터 밖에서도 볼 수 있어요.

4. A butterfly _________ with its _________.
   나비는 더듬이로 냄새를 맡아요.

5. There are _________ in my house.
   우리 집에 모기들이 있어요.

6. Some animals have _________ _________.
   어떤 동물들은 뛰어난 감각을 가지고 있어요.

7. I can also _________ very high and have a _________ _________ to catch things.

나는 매우 높게 점프할 수도 있고 끈적한 혀로 물건들을 잡을 수도 있어.

8. Hi. I'm Felix the Frog. I am a _________.

안녕. 나는 개구리 펠릭스야. 나는 슈퍼히어로야.

9. I wear a blue _________ and a red _________.

나는 파란 마스크와 빨간 망토를 두르고 있지.

10. Late one night, someone _________, "Help me!"

어느 늦은 밤, 누군가가 "도와주세요!"라고 소리를 질렀어.

11. Can you _________ with your whole body?

여러분은 온몸으로 맛을 느낄 수 있나요?

12. You can _________ meat cooking on a _________ from 10 meters.

여러분은 10 미터 밖에서 바비큐 그릴에서 요리되는 고기의 냄새를 맡을 수 있어요.

13. A butterfly has _________ _________.

나비는 겹눈을 가지고 있어요.

14. Wow! What _________ _________!

와! 정말로 놀라운 생명체들이에요!

15. A butterfly doesn't have a _________.

나비는 혀가 없어요.

16. I have a super _________ _________ _________.

나는 뛰어난 시각을 가지고 있어.

17. With my super sense of sight, I _________ _________.

나의 뛰어난 시각으로 나는 주위를 둘러보았어.

18. I can _________ high sounds _________ my ears and low sounds _________ my skin.

나는 고음을 귀를 통해 들을 수 있고 저음을 피부를 통해 들을 수 있어.

19. It _________ sound with the hairs on its _________.

나비는 날개들에 달린 털로 소리를 느껴요.

20. _________ _________ _________, who are you?

그런데, 당신은 누구지요?

C **Listen to the passage and fill in the blanks.**

Lesson 1 Animals with Super Senses 🎧 01

Some animals have __________ __________. Their senses are much __________ than ours.

You taste with your __________. Can you taste with your whole body? A __________ tastes with its whole body. It can even taste with its __________. A catfish has a super __________ __________ __________.

You __________ with your eyes. How far can you see? You can see a __________ mouse from 10 meters. A __________ can see the same mouse __________ 1,500 meters. A falcon has a super sense of __________.

You smell with your __________. You can smell __________ cooking on a barbecue from 10 meters. A __________ can smell meat from 1,000 meters. A wolf has a super __________ __________ __________.

A __________ has many super senses. A butterfly has __________ eyes. It can see in all directions without __________ its head. A butterfly has a super sense of __________.

A butterfly doesn't have a __________. Then how does it smell? It smells with its __________. A butterfly has a __________ __________ of __________.

A butterfly __________ have a tongue. Then how does it taste? It tastes with its __________. A butterfly's sense of __________ is one of its super senses. A butterfly doesn't have __________. Then how does it __________? It feels sound with the __________ on its wings. It has a super sense of __________.

Wow! What __________ creatures! Unlike us, they have many __________ __________.

Lesson 2 **A Superhero** 🎧 **02**

Hi. I'm Felix the Frog. I am a __________. I wear a blue mask and a red __________.

I have __________ super senses. I have a super sense of __________. I have big eyes

that can see all __________ me. They are on the top of my head, so I don't need to

__________ my head to look around! I have a __________ __________ of __________.

I can hear high __________ __________ my ears and low sounds through my

__________. I have a super sense of __________. I can find things by __________.

I can also jump very high and have a __________ ____ ___ to catch things. These

are not super senses, but they __________ me as a __________.

Late one night, someone __________, "Help me!"

The sound was coming __________ an old house. Inside the house was a girl.

"Help me, please!" she cried. "There are __________ in my house. They are too small,

and I __________ see them. They are __________ me."

"Mosquitoes? No problem! I can find them," I said.

With my __________ __________ __________ __________, I looked around. She was

right. There were many mosquitoes. I __________ the mosquitoes with my super

sense of smell. Then, I ________ around as high as I could. Using my __________

__________, I began to eat the mosquitoes. Soon, all the mosquitoes __________

__________.

"Oh, thank you. You helped me. __________ __________ __________, who are you?"

asked the girl.

"I am Felix. I like to __________ people," I said.

"Wow, you are a real __________," she said.

What Does It Look Like?

A Write the words and phrases in English or Korean.

1.	피부		11.	take a look at	
2.	발톱		12.	spend	
3.	이빨들		13.	eat up	
4.	냉혈의		14.	deadly	
5.	먹이, 사냥감		15.	under	
6.	용		16.	inside	
7.	무게가 나가다		17.	crack	
8.	비늘이 있는		18.	different	
9.	파충류		19.	wing	
10.	물다, 물어뜯다		20.	behind	

B Complete the sentences.

1. This animal has dry __________.
   이 동물은 건조한 피부를 가지고 있어요.

2. When it hunts, it doesn't use its __________.
   그것은 사냥할 때 발톱들을 사용하지 않아요.

3. This animal has a big mouth and __________ __________.
   이 동물은 커다란 입과 날카로운 이빨을 가지고 있어요.

4. They __________ eggs and are __________________.
   그것들은 알을 낳고 냉혈동물이에요.

5. When it __________ in the water, it can catch its __________.
   이 동물은 물속에 숨어 있을 때도 먹이를 잡을 수 있어요.

6. These animals are not real __________.
   이러한 동물들은 진짜 용들은 아니에요.

7. It can __________ __________ to 3 meters long and __________ up to 70 kilograms.
이 동물은 3미터 정도까지 자라며 몸무게는 70 킬로그램 정도까지 나가요.

8. It has __________ skin.
그것은 비늘로 덮인 피부를 가지고 있어요.

9. These animals are __________.
이 동물들은 파충류예요.

10. When it __________ animals, they can become __________ and die.
이 동물이 다른 동물들을 물면 그 동물들은 아프게 되어 죽어버릴 수 있어요.

11. Let's __________ a closer __________ __________ them.
그것들을 더 자세히 살펴봅시다.

12. It __________ most of its time in the water.
이 동물은 대부분의 시간을 물속에서 보내요.

13. When it eats, it can __________ __________ to 80 percent of its body weight.
이 동물이 먹이를 먹을 때 자기 몸무게의 80퍼센트 정도까지 먹어치울 수 있답니다.

14. It has __________ bacteria inside its mouth.
이 동물의 입 속에는 치명적인 박테리아가 있어요.

15. Deep in a green forest, an egg is __________ a tree.
울창한 숲 안쪽에 알 하나가 나무 아래에 있어요.

16. Shh! Something is moving __________ the egg.
쉬! 알 안에서 무언가가 움직이고 있어요.

17. Small __________ push through the __________, and the egg opens.
작은 발톱들이 갈라진 금을 밀고 알이 열려요.

18. It looks like a __________ but is __________.
생김새는 파충류처럼 생겼지만 파충류와는 달라요.

19. Sure! I can fly with my __________.
물론이지! 나는 나의 날개들로 날 수가 있어.

20. Just then, it comes out from __________ the rock.
바로 그때, 그것이 바위 뒤에서 나와요.

Lesson 1 **Are They Dragons?** 🎧 03

Look at these animals. Are they __________ or not? Let's take a __________ look at them.

This animal has a __________ __________ and __________ __________. It likes to eat meat. This animal has dry, __________ skin and long claws. When it hunts, it doesn't use its __________. It opens its mouth wide to eat large __________. It spends most of its time in the water. Can you see its eyes on the __________ __________ its head? When it __________ in the water, it can still see and catch its __________. It can grow up to 4 meters long and __________ __________ __________ 453 kilograms.

Look at this animal. It __________ most of its time on dry land. It is very big, but it can run __________ __________. It can grow up to 3 meters long and __________ up to 70 kilograms. This animal has dry, scaly skin. It __________ __________ __________ meat. It __________ its long claws to __________ __________. When it eats, it can __________ up to 80 percent of its body weight. It has __________ bacteria inside its mouth. This means that when it __________ animals, they can become __________ __________ __________.

These animals __________ __________ dragons, but they are not __________ dragons. They are reptiles. __________ lay eggs and are __________. This means that they need the sun to stay warm. One is an alligator. The other is a Komodo dragon. Can you __________ which ones they are?

Lesson 2 Have You Ever Seen a Dragon Fly? 04

_________ in a green forest, an egg is _________ a tree. The egg is big and yellow.

What _________ of egg is it?

Shh! Something is moving _________ the egg. It wants to _________ _________.

The egg begins to _________. Something is using its claws to come _________ of

the egg. Small claws _________ _________ the crack, and the egg opens. Aha! It is a

dragon egg.

A baby _________ comes out of the egg. The baby dragon is purple. It has claws

and _________ _________. It has a long, hard tail. It looks like a _________ but is

_________. The baby dragon has two big _________.

At that same time, a boy named Daniel is walking in the green _________.

He hears a _________ sound. He sees something _________ _________ _________ of

a rock.

"Hmm… What is that? It looks like a _________," says Daniel.

 Just then, a baby dragon comes out from _________ the rock.

"Oh my! You're a _________. You're so cute. What's your name?" asks Daniel.

The baby dragon does not say _________. It just looks at Daniel.

"Umm. Dio! I'll name you Dio. Dio, _________ _________ _________?" says Daniel.

Dio says, "Sure! I can fly with my _________. Come and ride on me. Where do you

want me to fly?"

Daniel _________ on the dragon and says, "Fly wherever you want. But don't

_________ any trees!"

The dragon _________ _________ the trees, _________ the forest, and up to the

clouds. Daniel has a big _________.

Different Looks

A Write the words and phrases in English or Korean.

1. 땋은 머리
2. 대머리의, 머리가 벗겨진
3. 코밑수염, 콧수염
4. 근육
5. 아주 짧게 깎은 머리, 까까머리
6. 보조개, 움푹 들어간 곳
7. 따끔거리는, 가려운
8. 염색하다
9. 미용사, 헤어 디자이너
10. 비명을 지르다, 괴성을 지르다

11. different looks
12. light skin
13. messy
14. neither ~ nor ...
15. wrinkle
16. sibling
17. shiny
18. curly
19. sound asleep
20. switch

B Complete the sentences.

1. Jenny's hair is long and straight. And she has __________.
   제니의 머리는 긴 생머리예요. 그리고 그녀는 땋은 머리를 하고 있어요

2. He is the __________ of Mark's school. He is a short man with a __________ head.
   그는 마크가 다니는 학교의 교장선생님이에요. 그는 키가 작고 대머리예요.

3. He has a thin __________.   그는 가는 콧수염을 갖고 있어요.

4. He is __________ and has a lot of __________ on his body.
   그는 힘이 세고 몸에는 근육이 많아요.

5. He is Mark's __________ __________ teacher. He has a __________ __________.
   그는 마크의 체육 선생님이에요. 그는 아주 짧게 깎은 머리를 하고 있어요.

6. She has a __________ when she smiles.

그녀는 웃을 때는 보조개가 있어요.

7. It looks __________.   그것은 따가워 보여요.

8. Also, he wants to __________ his hair red.

또한 그는 그의 머리 색을 빨강색으로 염색하고 싶어해요.

9. At the __________ __________, Reg and Shirley meet Joan, the __________.

미용실에서 레지와 셜리는 헤어 디자이너인 조앤을 만나요.

10. "Ahhhhhhhh!" __________ Shirley.   "으아아아아아악!" 셜리가 비명을 질러요.

11. People have __________ __________. Look at the people __________ you.

사람마다 다른 생김새들을 가지고 있어요. 여러분 주위의 사람들을 보세요.

12. He has __________ __________. His eyes are big and __________.

그는 밝은색 피부를 갖고 있어요. 그의 눈은 크고 파란색이에요.

13. He really likes to __________, so he is __________.

그는 물감으로 그림 그리기를 정말로 좋아해서 지저분해요.

14. He is __________ tall nor short. He also has a __________ smile.

그는 키가 크지도 않고 작지도 않아요. 그는 또한 매력적인 미소를 가지고 있어요.

15. He has __________ on his __________ and always __________ __________ students over his glasses.

그의 이마에는 주름살이 있고 항상 안경 너머로 학생들을 쳐다봐요.

16. Reg and Shirley are __________. They are twins, so they __________ __________.

레지와 셜리는 남매예요. 그늘은 쌍둥이라서 같아보여요.

17. They both have __________ brown hair. And they both have __________ __________ __________.

그들은 모두 윤기 나는 갈색 머리카락을 가지고 있어요. 그리고 둘 다 아주 밝은 미소를 가지고 있어요.

18. Shirley thinks __________ __________ looks good, so she wants a __________.

셜리는 곱슬머리가 좋다고 생각해서 퍼머를 하기를 원해요.

19. Sitting in the chairs, they feel sleepy. Soon, they are __________ __________.

의자에 앉아 있는 동안 레지와 셜리는 졸음이 와요. 곧 그들은 깊이 잠이 들어요.

20. She made a __________. She __________ their hairstyles.

그녀는 실수를 했어요. 그녀는 그들의 헤어스타일을 뒤바꿔버렸어요.

C **Listen to the passage and fill in the blanks.**

Lesson 1 **How Do They Look?** 05

People have _________ ________. Look at the people around you. How do they look? _________ take a closer _________ at some other people.

Look at Mark. He has light skin. His _________ are big and blue. His hair is _________ and _________. He has a _________ _________ and thin lips. He really likes to paint, so he is _________.

Look at Jenny. She is Mark's _________ friend. Her skin is neither _________ nor light. Her eyes are brown and small. Jenny's hair is long and _________. And she has _________. She has _________ when she smiles.

Look at John. He is the _________ of Mark's school. He is a short man with a _________ head. He has a thin _________ that looks _________. He has _________ on his forehead and always looks at students over his _________.

Look at Michael. He is Mark's Physical Education teacher. He has a _________ _________. He is strong and has a lot of _________ on his body. His shoulders are very big. He is _________ tall nor short. He also has a _________ smile.

People _________ _________ you can look different, but they can look nice. Think of some people you know. What do they _________ _________? What about you? What do you look _________? When you look in the mirror, _________ _________: How do I look?

D Listen to the story and fill in the blanks.

Reg and Shirley are __________. They are __________, so they look alike. They both have light skin and big blue eyes. They both have __________ __________ __________. And they both have __________ __________ __________. Even their voices are similar, so people cannot tell __________ __________ __________.

Today, Reg and Shirley are going to a __________ __________. They want __________ hairstyles. Reg thinks __________ __________ looks good, so he wants a __________ __________. Also, he wants to __________ his hair red. Red is his __________ color.

Shirley thinks curly hair looks good, so she wants a __________. She wants her hair to be __________, just like her favorite singer. Reg and Shirley are __________ about their new __________.

At the hair salon, Reg and Shirley meet Joan, the __________. Reg tells Joan he wants short red hair. Shirley tells Joan she wants __________ hair.

"__________ __________," says Joan. "Come and sit down."

Joan __________ Reg and Shirley in large gowns to keep them clean. Sitting in the chairs, Reg and Shirley feel __________. Soon, they are __________ asleep.

Joan begins to cut their hair. Buzz, buzz, buzz. Snip, snip, snip. She styles the twins' hair. After a while, she is __________.

"Okay. I'm done. Open your eyes, kids," says Joan.

"Ahhhhhhhh!" __________ Shirley. "Noooooooo!" screams Reg.

"What's __________?" asks Joan. "Don't you like your hairstyles?"

As Joan takes the gowns off Reg and Shirley, she sees the problem. She __________ __________ __________. She __________ their hairstyles. Joan looks at Reg. He has a beautiful curly __________. Joan looks at Shirley. She has a beautiful red __________ __________.

"Oh, no!" says Joan.

Helpful Plants

A **Write the words and phrases in English or Korean.**

1.	약, 약물		11.	in many ways
2.	목화, 면, 솜		12.	come from
3.	열, 고열		13.	be made of
4.	하이킹하다, 도보여행을 하다		14.	heal
5.	지팡이		15.	root
6.	꽉 막힌 코		16.	lunchtime
7.	(야영장의) 모닥불		17.	climb
8.	배탈, 복통		18.	all day long
9.	도움이 되는, 유익한		19.	not ~ anymore
10.	다치게 하다, 아프게 하다		20.	next to

B **Complete the sentences.**

1. Some plants are used as __________. When you are sick, some plants can make you __________ __________.
   어떤 식물들은 약으로 사용돼요. 여러분이 아플 때 어떤 식물들은 여러분의 기분을 더 낫게 만들어 줄 수 있어요.

2. Some clothes are made of __________. __________ comes from a plant.
   어떤 옷들은 목화로 만들어져요. 목화도 식물에서 나오지요.

3. If you have a __________, eat or drink some ginger. It helps cool your __________.
   만약 열이 난다면 생강을 먹거나 마셔봐요. 열을 내리는 데 도움이 된답니다.

4. She likes to __________ in the __________.
   그녀는 정글에서 하이킹하는 것을 좋아해요.

5. Jen found a good __________ __________.
   그녀는 좋은 지팡이를 찾았어요.

6. If you have a ___________ ___________, try some mint.

코가 막혔을 때는 박하를 사용해봐요.

7. She wanted to make a ___________. She ___________ ___________ some wood.

그녀는 모닥불을 피우고 싶었죠. 그녀는 나무를 찾아보았어요.

8. If you have a ___________, drink some ginger in tea or juice.

만약 배가 아프다면 생강차나 생강주스를 마셔봐요.

9. Aloe vera is a very ___________ plant. People make ___________ ___________ with aloe vera.

알로에 베라는 매우 도움이 되는 식물이에요. 사람들은 알로에 베라로 도움이 되는 것들을 만들어요.

10. If you ___________ your skin, put some aloe gel on it.

피부에 상처가 나면 알로에 젤을 발라봐요.

11. Plants help you ___________ ___________ ___________.

식물들은 여러 가지 방법으로 여러분을 도와줘요.

12. Watermelon, potatoes, and carrots ___________ ___________ plants.

수박, 감자, 당근은 식물에서 나와요.

13. Paper, tissue, and toys are ___________ ___________ wood.

종이, 티슈, 그리고 장난감은 목재로 만들어져요.

14. Jen was happy because the plant ___________ her ___________.

알로에 베라 식물이 그녀의 상처를 치료했기 때문에 젠은 행복했어요.

15. ___________ is another plant. Ginger is a ___________.

생강은 또 다른 식물이에요. 생강은 뿌리예요.

16. It was ___________. Jungle Jen felt ___________, so she found a mango tree.

점심시간이었어요. 정글 젠은 배가 고파서 망고나무를 찾았어요.

17. Jen ___________ the big rock. But she fell down.

젠은 그 큰 바위를 기어올랐어요. 하지만 그녀는 떨어졌어요.

18. After eating, Jungle Jen ___________ in the jungle ___________ ___________ ___________.

먹은 후에 정글 젠은 하루 종일 정글 속을 걸었어요.

19. She didn't feel tired ___________.   그녀는 더 이상 피곤함을 느끼지 않았어요.

20. She was warm and felt ___________ ___________ ___________ the campfire.

그녀는 모닥불 옆에서 따뜻해졌고 졸렸어요.

C Listen to the passage and fill in the blanks.

Lesson 1 How Do Plants Help You? 07

_________ help you in _________ _________. How do plants help you?
You _________ food every day. Plants give you food to eat. Watermelon, potatoes,
and carrots _________ _________ plants. You wear clothes. Look at your clothes. Are
they _________ _________ cotton? Some clothes are _________ of cotton. _________
comes from a plant. Paper, tissue, and toys are made of _________. Wood comes
from trees.
Some plants are used as _________. When you are _________, some plants can
make you feel better. If you have a _________ _________, try some mint. It helps
clear your nose.
Aloe vera is a very _________ plant. It is green and _________. People make helpful
things with aloe vera. If you _________ your skin, put some aloe gel on it. It helps
_________ your skin. If your skin is dry, _________ some aloe cream on it. Your
_________ will not feel dry. If you are dirty, wash with aloe _________. Aloe soap
helps clean your skin.
_________ is another helpful plant. Ginger is a root. If you have a _________,
drink some ginger in _________ _________ _________. It helps _________ your
stomach. If you have a _________, eat or drink some ginger. It helps _________ your
fever. Ginger can also _________ _________ _________ food or candy.
Plants are helpful in your life. They _________ you food, clothes, medicine, and
many _________ _________.

D **Listen to the story and fill in the blanks.**

Lesson 2 **A Girl Named Jungle Jen** 🎧 08

Please meet the girl, Jungle Jen. Do you know __________ her name is Jungle Jen?

She __________ __________ __________ in the jungle.

One day, Jungle Jen was __________ in the jungle. She saw a big rock. Jen __________

the big rock. But she __________ __________. She hurt her hand. She needed some

__________ to put on her hand.

Jen looked for an __________ __________ plant. When she __________ one, she put

aloe gel on her hand. Soon, her hand did not hurt __________.

Jen was happy because the plant __________ __________ __________.

It was __________. Jungle Jen felt hungry, so she found a mango tree. Jen loves to eat

mangoes. Soon, she was not __________ anymore.

__________ eating, Jungle Jen walked in the jungle __________ __________ __________.

She felt __________. She __________ __________ a stick. Jen found a good __________

__________. She didn't feel tired anymore.

That __________, Jungle Jen began to get cold. She wanted to make a __________.

She looked __________ some __________. When she found some, Jen made a

__________. She was warm and felt sleepy __________ __________ the campfire. She

wanted to sleep. She looked for some big __________. When she found some, she

made a __________ bed.

That night, Jungle Jen __________ very well. She was happy to have many __________

__________ in the jungle.

Unique Food from around the World

A Write the words and phrases in English or Korean.

1.	곤충		11.	unique
2.	벌레		12.	explain
3.	튀긴 음식		13.	popular
4.	밥 한 뭉치		14.	as ~ as ...
5.	간식		15.	grasshopper
6.	장식하다		16.	special
7.	맛, 풍미		17.	cockroach
8.	재료, 성분		18.	protein
9.	담그다, 퍼내다		19.	be interested in
10.	바삭바삭한		20.	beetle

B Complete the sentences.

1. I __________ some dishes made with __________.
   저는 곤충들로 만든 음식들을 조사했어요.

2. Mariko picked up the __________.
   마리코가 벌레들을 집어 들었어요.

3. From the kitchen, we smelled __________ __________.
   우리는 부엌에서 나는 튀김 냄새를 맡았어요.

4. The insects are fried in __________, and then they are put on a __________ __________ __________.
   곤충들을 기름에 튀긴 후에 뭉쳐놓은 밥 위에 올려놓아요.

5. This food is a __________ __________ that kids like.
   이 음식은 아이들이 좋아하는 달콤한 간식이에요.

6. ___________, she ___________ them with yellow and pink flowers and green leaves.
마지막으로, 그녀는 노란색과 분홍색의 꽃들과 초록색 나뭇잎으로 장식을 했어요.

7. Then, ___________ and herbs are added for ___________.
그런 다음에, 마늘과 허브를 넣어서 향미를 내요.

8. Let's get some ___________ for more food.   음식을 더 만들기 위해 재료들을 더 가지러 가자.

9. At other times, they are ___________ in salt.   어떨 때는 소금에 담겨지기도 해요.

10. They are ___________ and ___________ good.   이 음식은 바삭거리고 좋은 맛이 나요.

11. Write about some of the ___________ dishes that people eat ___________ ___________ ___________.
전 세계 사람들이 먹는 독특한 음식에 대해서 적어보세요.

12. Then, ___________ how they are cooked.
그런 다음, 그것들이 어떻게 요리되는지 설명해보세요.

13. In Cambodia, a ___________ ___________ is deep ___________ tarantula.
캄보디아에서 인기 있는 요리는 튀긴 타란툴라예요.

14. Tarantulas are ___________ ___________ ___________ an adult's palm.
타란툴라는 거의 어른 손바닥 크기만큼 커요.

15. The ___________ are as long ___________ a finger.   메뚜기는 손가락 길이만 해요.

16. In Japan, some people use ___________ ___________ ___________ insects to make a ___________ sushi.
일본에서 몇몇 일본 사람들은 특별한 초밥을 만들기 위해서 여러 종류의 곤충들을 사용해요.

17. They ___________ select insects like ___________, bees, and ___________.
그들은 바퀴벌레들, 벌, 그리고 전갈들과 같은 곤충들을 조심스럽게 골라요.

18. These days, we have to ___________ lots of cows and pigs to get ___________.
오늘날, 우리는 단백질을 얻기 위해서 많은 소와 돼지를 길러야만 해요.

19. We ___________ both ___________ in trying them.
우리 둘은 그것들을 먹어보는 것이 흥미로웠어요.

20. ___________ the rock were ___________, ___________, and spiders.
돌 밑에는 딱정벌레들, 벌레들, 그리고 거미들이 있었어요.

 Listen to the passage and fill in the blanks.

Lesson 1 What Unique Food! 09

Name: Charlie   Date: May 7

Instructions: Write about some of the __________ __________ that people eat

__________ __________ __________. Then, __________ how they are cooked.

I __________ some unique dishes made with insects around the world. They are as

__________:

1. Name of the Food: Deep Fried Tarantula   *Country: Cambodia*

In Cambodia, a __________ dish is deep fried tarantula. Tarantulas are large spiders.

They are __________ __________ __________ an adult's palm. This food is a __________

__________ that kids like. The __________ are fried in oil and sometimes are __________

__________ sugar. At other times, they are __________ in salt. They taste like chicken

and potato chips.

2. Name of the Food: Crunchy Grasshopper   *Country: Thailand*

In Thailand, people like eating __________ grasshoppers. The grasshoppers are _____

__________ __________ a finger. First, they fry the __________ in oil. Then, __________

and __________ are added for __________. They are crunchy and __________ good.

3. Name of the Food: Insect Sushi   *Country: Japan*

In Japan, some people use __________ __________ __________ insects to make a

__________ __________. They carefully select insects like __________, bees, and

__________. The insects are fried in oil, and then they are put on __________

__________ __________ __________. The crunchy fried insects with the sweet and sour

rice make a wonderful taste.

People think insects are __________ and __________. In fact, insects are full of

__________. These days, we have to __________ lots of cows and pigs to get

__________. But we don't need to raise insects. They can be a perfect food __________.

How about trying some insects as a __________ food?

Lesson 2 **Lunch with Mariko** 🎧 10

Mariko was the nicest __________ in our village. She always had a smile __________

__________ __________. One day, she __________ my friend Thomas and me to lunch.

We were excited. We __________ what she would cook.

We arrived for lunch __________ __________. "Welcome, boys. Lunch is almost ready,"

she said.

From the kitchen, we smelled __________ __________. It smelled great. We watched

Mariko cook. __________, Mariko fried some things in oil. They were __________

and __________. Next, she fried some large and black __________. She put them on

__________ __________ __________ __________. They looked like __________. Last, she

__________ them with yellow and pink flowers and green __________.

"Okay, boys. Try these first. If you like them, I'll make __________," said Mariko.

We were both __________ __________ trying them. I said, "Okay, Thomas. You eat the

black one, and I'll eat the brown one. Are you ready? On the __________ of three:

one, two, three."

__________! __________! We both ate them. I looked at Thomas. I saw his eyes open

wide. A large smile __________ on his face. He liked the sushi. And I liked it, too.

"So, boys, do you like them?" asked Mariko.

"More, please," we said.

"Sure! Let's get some __________ for more food," said Mariko.

We __________ Mariko outside. She walked to some green bushes. She __________

__________ a large rock. Under the rock were __________, __________, and __________.

Mariko picked up the bugs and __________. Thomas and I were __________. She had

cooked them for lunch. Eww!

An Amazing Story

A Write the words and phrases in English or Korean.

1.	돌고래		11.	digest
2.	플라스틱		12.	stomach
3.	수족관		13.	wrap
4.	호루라기, 호각		14.	trainer
5.	묘기, 재주		15.	tweet
6.	놀라운		16.	flipper
7.	삼키다		17.	backflip
8.	똑똑한, 영리한		18.	volunteer
9.	없애다, 치우다		19.	splash
10.	목숨을 구하다		20.	soak

B Complete the sentences.

1. The __________ became very weak.
그 돌고래들은 아주 약해졌어요.

2. There was __________ in the pool.
수영장에는 플라스틱이 있었어요.

3. Two __________ were swimming in an __________.
돌고래 두 마리가 수족관에서 수영을 하고 있었어요.

4. I trained them with my __________.
저는 그들을 제 호각으로 훈련시켰어요.

5. When they hear my __________, they do __________.
그들이 제 호각 소리를 들으면 재주를 부린답니다.

6. Do you want to hear an __________ story?
여러분은 정말 놀라운 이야기를 듣고 싶나요?

7. They __________ some.

그들은 조금 삼켰어요.

8. They are very __________.

그것들은 매우 영리하답니다.

9. They tried to __________ it. But they __________.

그들은 그것을 빼내려고 시도를 했어요. 하지만 실패했지요.

10. The worker __________ Bao, and he __________ to help __________ the dolphins.

조련사는 바오에게 전화를 했고, 바오는 돌고래들을 구하는 일을 도와주는 데 동의했어요.

11. But they couldn't __________ it.

하지만 그들은 그것을 소화할 수 없었어요.

12. It hurt their __________.

이것이 그들의 위장을 아프게 했지요.

13. Then, they __________ towels around the dolphins' __________.

그런 다음에 수건으로 돌고래의 이빨들을 감쌌어요.

14. I am a __________.

저는 조련사예요.

15. Watch. __________! They come to my __________.

보세요. 호르륵! 그들이 제 옆쪽으로 오지요.

16. They __________ their __________ at you.

그들이 여러분에게 지느러미를 흔드네요.

17. Jump high in the air and do a __________.

공중으로 높게 점프한 후 뒤로 공중돌기를 해라.

18. This will be my __________' best __________. I need a __________.

이번 묘기가 돌고래들의 최고의 묘기가 될 거예요. 지원자가 필요해요.

19. They're coming __________ at me. They __________ high in the air... __________!

그들이 저에게로 곧바로 오네요. 그들이 공중으로 높이 점프를 하네요… 첨벙!

20. They __________ me with water. Let's __________ __________ the card.

그들이 저를 완전히 물에 젖게 만드네요. 자, 카드를 볼까요.

Lesson 1 Lucky Dolphins 🎧 11

Do you want to hear an __________ story?

It all began in the town of Fushun, China. Two __________ were swimming in an

__________. There was __________ in the pool, and they __________ some. But the

dolphins couldn't __________ the plastic. The plastic __________ their __________.

Soon, they stopped __________ their food. The workers were __________. They tried

to __________ the plastic from their stomachs. But they __________. The dolphins

became very __________. If the plastic could not be __________, the dolphins would

die.

One of the __________ had an idea. He remembered Bao Xishun, the world's

__________ man. He was 2.36 meters tall, and his __________ were 1.06 meters long.

The worker thought that Bao could __________ the dolphins. He could __________

inside the dolphins' __________ with his long arms. Then, he could __________

__________ the plastic. The worker called Bao, and he __________ to help save the

dolphins. Workers opened the dolphins' __________. Then, they __________ towels

around the dolphins' teeth. Now the dolphins' teeth couldn't __________ Bao.

With his long arms, Bao reached __________ the dolphins' stomachs. He __________

out the plastic. Bao __________ the dolphins.

Today, the dolphins are happy again. Many people __________ __________ __________

them in their aquarium. And it is all __________ __________ the world's tallest man.

__________ an amazing story!

D **Listen to the story and fill in the blanks.**

Lesson 2 **Those Amazing Dolphins!** 🎧 12

Hello, everyone. My name is Dave. I am a dolphin __________ at this __________. My dolphins are very __________. I trained them with my __________. When they hear my whistle, they __________ __________. Watch. __________! The dolphins come to my __________. Tweet, tweet! They wave their __________ at you. Everyone, say hello to my __________ dolphins.

I also __________ my dolphins to read. I will show them this card. My lovely dolphins, read the __________ on this card.

● Jump high __________ __________ __________ and do a __________.

Now, show me the trick. Watch the dolphins swim off like __________ __________ __________ lighting. Look how they jump __________ in the air and do a backflip. Everyone, are you __________ the show? This time, I will not blow my __________. Shh! Everybody, this will be my dolphins' __________ __________. I need a __________. Over there! The boy with a red shirt. What about you? Can you write some __________ on this card? Thank you! Shh~~! This time, I will not __________ it to the dolphins. Dolphins, __________ us the tricks that are __________ on the card. Look! They jump through __________ __________. Wait. Where are they going? They're coming __________ __________ __________. They jump high in the air... __________! Oh, my gosh! They __________ me with water.

Let's look at the card.

● Jump __________ two hoops. Then, __________ Dave with water.

Look! They did the tricks __________ reading the card. Oh, those __________ dolphins!

Beyond Words

A Write the words and phrases in English or Korean.

1.	손동작들	11.	meaning
2.	찰싹 때리다	12.	thumb
3.	경기장, 스타디움	13.	more than
4.	검, 칼	14.	push one's way through the crowd
5.	창, 작살	15.	soldier
6.	긍정적인	16.	salute
7.	검투사	17.	arrive
8.	관중, 청중	18.	fight
9.	축하하다	19.	cheer
10.	의사소통하다	20.	decide

B Complete the sentences.

1. __________ you use __________ __________ such as a high five or an okay sign.
   가끔 여러분은 하이 파이브나 오케이 사인과 같은 손동작들을 사용해요.

2. When a baseball player hit a homerun, another player raised his hand to __________ the player's hand in celebration.
   한 야구선수가 홈런을 쳤을 때, 다른 선수가 축하해 주려고 그 선수의 손을 찰싹 때리기 위해 손을 들었어요.

3. The first __________ __________ was done in 1977 at a baseball __________ in America.
   첫 번째 하이 파이브는 1977년 미국 야구 경기장에서 행해졌어요.

4. He has a __________ __________ __________ on his head. In his hand, he has a sharp __________.
   그는 커다란 금색 투구를 머리에 쓰고 있어. 손에는 날카로운 검을 들고 있어.

5. He has a __________ __________ on his face. In his hand, he has a __________ __________.
그는 은색 마스크를 얼굴에 쓰고 있어. 손에는 긴 창을 들고 있어.

6. __________ __________ means "well done" or "good job" and is a __________ sign.
엄지손가락을 세우는 것은 '잘했어요' 또는 '수고했어요'라는 의미이고, 긍정적인 신호예요.

7. They __________ on the life or death of a defeated __________.
그들은 싸움에서 진 검투사의 생사에 대해 투표를 했어요.

8. This gesture __________ __________ the __________ in the ancient Roman Coliseum.
이 동작은 고대 로마시대 콜로세움의 관중들에게서 나왔어요.

9. Now, people use this gesture to __________ something.
지금은 사람들이 어떤 일을 축하할 때 이 동작을 사용해요.

10. __________ __________ are a good way to __________.
손동작들은 의사소통하기에 좋은 수단이에요.

11. What are their __________, and where do they __________ __________?
그것들의 의미들은 무엇이고, 어디에서 왔을까요?

12. She closes her __________ with her __________ upward.
그녀는 엄지손가락들을 올린 채 두 주먹을 쥐어요.

13. Hand gestures can mean __________ __________ the words you __________.
손동작은 여러분이 말하는 단어들보다 더 많은 것을 의미할 수도 있어요.

14. There are so many people that we have to __________ our __________ __________ the crowd.
사람들이 너무 많아서 우리는 군중들 속에서 밀면서 가야 해요.

15. There are even Roman __________ there.
거기에는 로마 병사들도 있어요.

16. They are __________ each other.
그들은 서로에게 경례를 하고 있어요.

17. Finally, we __________. We look down at them.
마침내 우리는 도착해요. 우리는 그들을 내려다 보아요.

18. The __________ begins. They __________ well.
싸움이 시작돼요. 그들은 잘 싸워요.

19. __________, everyone in the __________ begins to __________.
갑자기, 모든 관중들이 환호하기 시작해요.

20. They are __________ __________ the audience to __________ if Maximus lives or dies.
그들은 막시무스를 살릴지 죽일지에 대해 관중들이 결정을 내리기를 기다리고 있어요.

Lesson 1 **Hand Gestures** 🎧 13

Sometimes you use __________ __________ such as a __________ __________ or an okay

sign. When do you use them? Why do you use them? What are their __________,

and where do they __________ __________?

Two boys __________ their hands and __________ __________. Then they hit their

__________ together. They might say, "High-five." This gesture takes its __________

from the five fingers on a hand and the raising of hands __________. The first high

five was done in 1977 at a __________ __________ in America. When a Los Angeles

baseball player hit a __________, another player raised his hand to __________ the

player's hand in celebration. Now, people use this gesture to __________ something.

A cute girl shows __________ __________. She closes her fists with her __________

upward. Thumbs up means "__________ __________" or "good job" and is a

__________ sign. This gesture comes from the audience in the __________ Roman

Coliseum. The audience __________ on the life or death of a __________ gladiator. A

__________ __________ gave life, and a thumbs down gave __________.

The scuba diver in the water gives the __________ __________ by making a circle with

two fingers. When you're eating food, it's __________ to talk with your mouth full.

__________ __________ __________, you can use it to mean "great" or "fine."

Hand gestures are a good way to __________. Hand gestures can mean more than

the __________ you speak. Think of some other gestures that you __________ use.

What do you think they mean? Where do they __________ __________?

D **Listen to the story and fill in the blanks.**

Lesson 2 **A Day at the Coliseum** 🎧 14

"Hey, Marcus," I shout. "Hurry up. Or we are going to __________ __________

__________."

My best friend Marcus and I are __________ to the Coliseum. We are going to see

the __________ fight. I don't want to be late. There are so many people that we have

to __________ our way __________ the __________. There are even Roman __________

there. They are __________ each other.

Finally, we __________. We look down at the gladiators. They are so big. And they

look very __________.

"Wow, Antony," says Marcus. "Look at Spartacus over there. He has __________

__________ __________ __________ on his head. In his hand, he has a sharp __________.

I hope he wins."

"No way," I tell Marcus. "I like Maximus. He has a __________ __________ on his face.

In his hand, he has a long __________. I hope he wins."

The __________ begins. Both gladiators fight well. The crowd is __________. They

are enjoying the fight. Marcus and I are __________ the fight, too. Soon, the fight

is __________. Spartacus, with the __________ helmet, fought very well. He won the

fight. Now, both gladiators stand __________ __________ __________ of the Coliseum.

They are __________ __________ the audience to __________ if Maximus lives or dies.

__________, everyone in the audience begins to __________. Marcus and I cheer, too.

Then, we all give the thumbs-up __________. Maximus fought well. We want him to

live.

__________ __________, Marcus and I are happy. What a great day at the Coliseum!

Spartacus and Maximus are both great __________. I __________ who will win the

__________ __________.

UNIT 8 — Science inside Balls

A. Write the words and phrases in English or Korean.

1.	실밥, 바늘땀		11.	lose
2.	유니폼, 제복		12.	catch
3.	작은 돌기, 혹 → (형) bumpy 울퉁불퉁한		13.	space
4.	잔털, 보풀 → (형) fuzzy 솜털이 보송보송한		14.	throw
5.	투수		15.	lost and found
6.	방향		16.	shelf
7.	표면		17.	in the air
8.	(공 등이) 튀다, 튀게 하다		18.	toward
9.	팀원, 같은 팀 동료		19.	kick
10.	꽉 잡다, 움켜잡다		20.	score

B. Complete the sentences.

1. When you __________ it, you can __________ the __________ on it.
네가 이 공을 던질 때, 공에 있는 바늘땀들을 느낄 수 있을 거야.

2. __________, Scott __________ __________ his blue __________.
첫 번째로 스콧은 그의 파란색 유니폼을 입어요.

3. Your basketball has small __________ on its surface.
너의 농구공 표면에는 작은 돌기들이 있어.

4. The __________ on a tennis ball helps the ball __________ on a racket.
테니스공의 보송보송한 털은 공이 라켓에서 튀는 데 도움을 줘.

5. __________ can __________ the baseball wherever they want.
투수들은 자기가 원하는 곳으로 야구공을 던질 수 있지.

6. The stitches on a __________ help it curve and change __________ in the air.

야구공에 있는 실밥은 공중에서 곡선으로 가거나 방향을 바꾸는 데 도움을 줘.

7. Your tennis ball has a __________ __________.

너의 테니스 공은 보송보송한 표면을 가지고 있구나.

8. Tennis players can __________ and __________ the ball well with a racket.

테니스 선수들은 라켓으로 공을 잘 튀기거나 회전을 시킬 수 있지.

9. His __________ passes him the ball.

그의 팀 동료가 공을 그에게 패스해줘요.

10. The small __________ help you __________ the ball well.

작은 돌기들은 네가 그 공을 잘 잡도록 도와줘.

11. I __________ my bag with four balls. __________ you __________ my balls?

나는 공이 4개가 들어있는 가방을 잃어버렸어. 내 공들을 본 적이 있니?

12. Now, the __________ cannot __________ the ball.

이제 골키퍼는 공을 잡을 수 없어요.

13. Can you __________ my questions in the __________ below?

아래 빈 공간들에 내 질문에 대해서 대답해 줄 수 있니?

14. Basketball players __________ it __________ __________ __________.

농구 선수들은 그것을 네트 속으로 던지거든.

15. I will __________ your balls at the __________ __________ __________.

내가 너의 공들을 분실물 센터에 놔 둘게.

16. Scott looks ___ __________ __________ the __________.

스콧은 선반 위를 찾아봐요.

17. The ball is high __________ __________ __________.

공은 공중에 높이 떠요.

18. He runs __________ the net.

그는 골대를 향해서 뛰어요.

19. Scott's teammate __________ the ball into the net.

스콧의 팀 동료가 공을 차서 골대에 넣어요.

20. Now, the __________ is 2-0.

이제 점수는 2대 0이에요.

Lesson 1 Missing Balls 15

Hi, everyone.

I __________ my bag with four balls. __________ __________ __________ my balls? If you have seen them, please __________ them to me. They are my balls.

My __________ is big and orange. When you hold it, it feels __________. My baseball is small, hard, and white. When you __________ it, you can feel the __________ on it.

My tennis ball is small, __________, and yellow. When you hold it, it feels __________.

Last, my soccer ball is __________ and round. When you __________ my soccer ball, it feels __________. I love my balls __________ __________. Please find my balls.

Thank you,

From Steven

Hi, Steven.

I found your bag on the playground. But I am __________ about your balls. Can you answer my __________ in the spaces __________?

Question 1: Your basketball has small __________ on its __________. Why?

→ The small bumps help you __________ __________ __________ well. Basketball players grip it in their hand and throw it __________ __________ __________.

Question 2: Your baseball has __________ __________ on it. Why?

→ The stitches on a baseball help it __________ and change __________ in the air. __________ can throw the baseball __________ they want.

Question 3: Your tennis ball has a __________ surface. Why?

→ The fuzz on a tennis ball helps the ball __________ on a racket. Tennis players can bounce and spin the ball well with a __________.

If you write your answers in the spaces correctly, I will __________ your balls at the __________ and found.

From Russell

D **Listen to the story and fill in the blanks.**

Lesson 2 Game Day  16

Scott plays on a soccer team. He is getting __________ _________ a game today.
First, Scott __________ _________ his blue _________. Then, he puts on his soccer
shoes. Next, he gets his bag. Last, he gets his soccer ball. Oh no! He _________ find
his soccer ball.
Scott looks __________ _________ _________ the shelf. His ball is not there. Scott
looks _________ the door, _________ _________ the locker, and _________ the
bench. It is not in those places either. Scott is feeling _________. Where could it be?
_________, Scott has an idea. He looks inside his bag. Aha! There is his ball. Now, he
can go to the game.
The soccer game __________ _________ the whistle. "Hey, over here," calls Scott.
He wants the ball. His _________ passes him the ball. The ball is high _________
_________ _________. Scott uses his head to _________ the ball into the net. It is a
_________!
"Yay," yells Scott.
The _________ is 1-0. They can win the game.
Scott has the ball. He runs __ _____ the net.
"Kick! Kick!" yell Scott's _________. But he does not kick the ball to the net because
the _________ is ready to catch the ball. Scott _________ the ball to a teammate.
Now, the goalkeeper cannot catch the ball. Scott's teammate _________ the ball
into the net. Now, the score is 2-0.
"Hooray, we _________," yells Scott.
The game is _________. Scott and his teammates are __________ _________ _________
the game.
Today is a wonderful day.

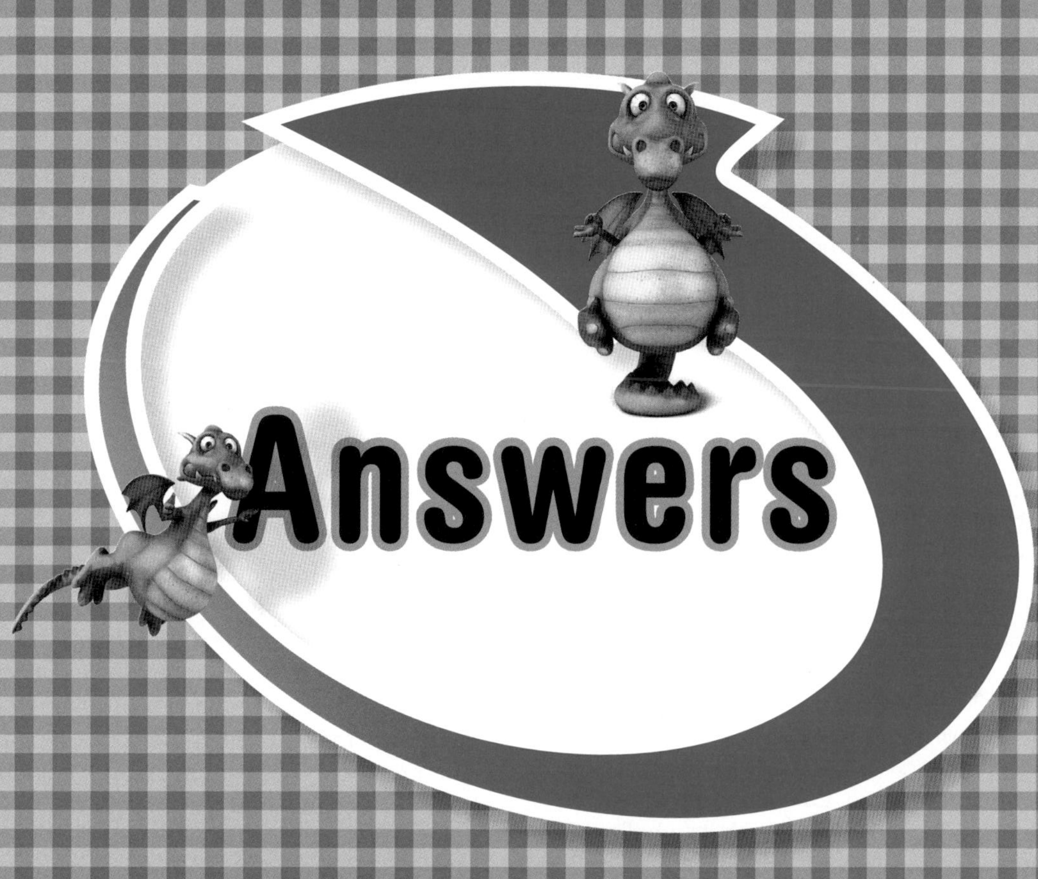

Answers

A 1. catfish   2. whisker
3. falcon   4. antennae
5. mosquito   6. super sense
7. sticky   8. superhero
9. cape   10. yell
11. 맛을 느끼다; 미각   12. 냄새 맡다
13. 겹눈   14. 생물, 창조물
15. 혀   16. 시각
17. 주위를 둘러보다   18. ~을 통하여
19. 느끼다   20. 그런데

B 1. catfish tastes   2. whiskers
3. falcon   4. smells / antennae
5. mosquitoes   6. super senses
7. jump / sticky tongue
8. superhero
9. mask / cape   10. yelled
11. taste   12. smell / barbecue
13. compound eyes   14. amazing creatures
15. tongue   16. sense of sight
17. looked around
18. hear / through / through
19. feels / wings   20. By the way

C   Lesson 1

Animals with Super Senses

Some animals have super senses. Their senses are much better than ours.
You taste with your tongue. Can you taste with your whole body? A catfish tastes with its whole body. It can even taste with its whiskers. A catfish has a super sense of taste.
You see with your eyes. How far can you see? You can see a small mouse from 10 meters. A falcon can see the same mouse from 1,500 meters. A falcon has a super sense of sight.
You smell with your nose. You can smell meat cooking on a barbecue from 10 meters. A wolf can smell meat from 1,000 meters. A wolf has a super sense of smell.
A butterfly has many super senses. A butterfly has compound eyes. It can see in all directions without turning its head. A butterfly has a super sense of sight. A butterfly doesn't have a nose. Then how does it smell? It smells with its antennae. A butterfly has a super sense of smell. A butterfly doesn't have a tongue. Then how does it taste? It tastes with its

feet. A butterfly's sense of taste is one of its super senses. A butterfly doesn't have ears. Then how does it hear? It feels sound with the hairs on its wings. It has a super sense of hearing.
Wow! What amazing creatures! Unlike us, they have many super senses.

D   Lesson 2

A Superhero

Hi. I'm Felix the Frog. I am a superhero. I wear a blue mask and a red cape.
I have three super senses. I have a super sense of sight. I have big eyes that can see all around me. They are on the top of my head, so I don't need to turn my head to look around! I have a super sense of hearing. I can hear high sounds through my ears and low sounds through my skin. I have a super sense of smell. I can find things by smelling.
I can also jump very high and have a sticky tongue to catch things. These are not super senses, but they help me as a superhero.
Late one night, someone yelled, "Help me!"
The sound was coming from an old house. Inside the house was a girl.
"Help me, please!" she cried. "There are mosquitoes in my house. They are too small, and I cannot see them. They are biting me."
"Mosquitoes? No problem! I can find them," I said.
With my super sense of sight, I looked around. She was right. There were many mosquitoes. I smelled the mosquitoes with my super sense of smell. Then, I jumped around as high as I could. Using my sticky tongue, I began to eat the mosquitoes. Soon, all the mosquitoes were gone.
"Oh, thank you. You helped me. By the way, who are you?" asked the girl.
"I am Felix. I like to help people," I said.
"Wow, you are a real superhero," she said.

38

A
1. skin
2. claw
3. teeth
4. cold-blooded
5. prey
6. dragon
7. weigh
8. scaly
9. reptile
10. bite
11. ~을 보다
12. 소비하다
13. 다 먹어치우다
14. 치명적인
15. ~ 아래에
16. ~ 안쪽에, 내부에
17. 갈라진 금; 금이 가다
18. 다른
19. 날개
20. ~ 뒤에

B
1. skin
2. claws
3. sharp teeth
4. lay / cold-blooded
5. hides / prey
6. dragons
7. grow up / weigh
8. scaly
9. reptiles
10. bites / sick
11. take / look at
12. spends
13. eat up
14. deadly
15. under
16. inside
17. claws / crack
18. reptile / different
19. wings
20. behind

C Lesson 1

Are They Dragons?

Look at these animals. Are they dragons or not? Let's take a closer look at them.
This animal has a big mouth and sharp teeth. It likes to eat meat. This animal has dry, scaly skin and long claws. When it hunts, it doesn't use its claws. It opens its mouth wide to eat large prey. It spends most of its time in the water. Can you see its eyes on the top of its head? When it hides in the water, it can still see and catch its prey. It can grow up to 4 meters long and weigh up to 453 kilograms.
Look at this animal. It spends most of its time on dry land. It is very big, but it can run very fast. It can grow up to 3 meters long and weigh up to 70 kilograms. This animal has dry, scaly skin. It likes to eat meat. It uses its long claws to hunt prey. When it eats, it can eat up to 80 percent of its body weight. It has deadly bacteria inside its mouth. This means that when it bites animals, they can become sick and die.
These animals look like dragons, but they are not real dragons. They are reptiles. Reptiles lay eggs and are cold-blooded. This means that they need the sun to stay warm. One is an alligator. The other is a Komodo dragon. Can you guess which ones they are?

D Lesson 2

Have You Ever Seen a Dragon Fly?

Deep in a green forest, an egg is under a tree. The egg is big and yellow. What kind of egg is it? Shh! Something is moving inside the egg. It wants to come out. The egg begins to crack. Something is using its claws to come out of the egg. Small claws push through the crack, and the egg opens. Aha! It is a dragon egg.
A baby dragon comes out of the egg. The baby dragon is purple. It has claws and scaly skin. It has a long, hard tail. It looks like a reptile but is different. The baby dragon has two big wings.
At that same time, a boy named Daniel is walking in the green forest. He hears a strange sound. He sees something around the corner of a rock. "Hmm… What is that? It looks like a tail," says Daniel.
Just then, a baby dragon comes out from behind the rock.
"Oh my! You're a dragon. You're so cute. What's your name?" asks Daniel.
The baby dragon does not say anything. It just looks at Daniel.
"Umm. Dio! I'll name you Dio. Dio, can you fly?" says Daniel.
Dio says, "Sure! I can fly with my wings. Come and ride on me. Where do you want me to fly?" Daniel gets on the dragon and says, "Fly wherever you want. But don't hit any trees!"
The dragon flies over the trees, above the forest, and up to the clouds. Daniel has a big smile.

3 UNIT — Different Looks

p.12

A
1. pigtail
2. bald
3. mustache
4. muscle
5. buzz cut
6. dimple
7. scratchy
8. dye
9. hairstylist
10. scream
11. 다른 생김새
12. 밝은색 피부
13. 지저분한, 엉망인
14. ~도 아니고 …도 아니다
15. 주름, 잔주름
16. 형제 자매
17. 빛나는, 윤기 나는
18. 곱슬머리의, 곱슬곱슬한
19. 깊이 잠든
20. 뒤바꾸다, 전환하다

B
1. pigtails
2. principal / bald
3. mustache
4. strong / muscles
5. Physical Education / buzz cut
6. dimple
7. scratchy
8. dye
9. hair salon / hairstylist
10. screams
11. different looks / around
12. light skin / blue
13. paint / messy
14. neither / charming
15. wrinkles / forehead / looks at
16. siblings / look alike
17. shiny / bright white smiles
18. curly hair / perm
19. sound asleep
20. mistake / switched

C

How Do They Look?

People have different looks. Look at the people around you. How do they look? Let's take a closer look at some other people.

Look at Mark. He has light skin. His eyes are big and blue. His hair is short and blond. He has a wide forehead and thin lips. He really likes to paint, so he is messy.

Look at Jenny. She is Mark's close friend. Her skin is neither dark nor light. Her eyes are brown and small. Jenny's hair is long and straight. And she has pigtails. She has dimples when she smiles.

Look at John. He is the principal of Mark's school. He is a short man with a bald head. He has a thin mustache that looks scratchy. He has wrinkles on his forehead and always looks at students over his glasses.

Look at Michael. He is Mark's Physical Education teacher. He has a buzz cut. He is strong and has a lot of muscles on his body. His shoulders are very big. He is neither tall nor short. He also has a charming smile.

People all around you can look different, but they can look nice. Think of some people you know. What do they look like? What about you? What do you look like? When you look in the mirror, ask yourself: How do I look?

D

Who Is Who?

Reg and Shirley are siblings. They are twins, so they look alike. They both have light skin and big blue eyes. They both have shiny brown hair. And they both have bright white smiles. Even their voices are similar, so people cannot tell who is who.

Today, Reg and Shirley are going to a hair salon. They want new hairstyles. Reg thinks short hair looks good, so he wants a buzz cut. Also, he wants to dye his hair red. Red is his favorite color. Shirley thinks curly hair looks good, so she wants a perm. She wants her hair to be curly, just like her favorite singer. Reg and Shirley are excited about their new hairstyles.

At the hair salon, Reg and Shirley meet Joan, the hairstylist. Reg tells Joan he wants short red hair. Shirley tells Joan she wants curly hair.

"No problem," says Joan. "Come and sit down." Joan covers Reg and Shirley in large gowns to keep them clean. Sitting in the chairs, Reg and Shirley feel sleepy. Soon, they are sound asleep.

Joan begins to cut their hair. Buzz, buzz, buzz. Snip, snip, snip. She styles the twins' hair. After a while, she is finished.

"Okay. I'm done. Open your eyes, kids," says Joan.

"Ahhhhhhhh!" screams Shirley.

"Noooooooo!" screams Reg.

"What's wrong?" asks Joan. "Don't you like your hairstyles?"

As Joan takes the gowns off Reg and Shirley, she sees the problem. She made a mistake. She switched their hairstyles. Joan looks at Reg. He has a beautiful curly perm. Joan looks at Shirley. She has a beautiful red buzz cut.

"Oh, no!" says Joan.

4 UNIT — Helpful Plants

p.16

A 1. medicine
2. cotton
3. fever
4. hike
5. walking stick
6. stuffed nose
7. campfire
8. stomachache
9. helpful
10. hurt
11. 많은 방법으로, 여러모로
12. ~에서 나오다, ~에서 생산되다
13. ~으로 만들어지다, ~으로 구성되다
14. 치유하다, 낫게 하다
15. 뿌리
16. 점심시간
17. 오르다, 올라가다
18. 하루 종일, 온종일
19. 더 이상 ~않다
20. ~ 옆에

B 1. medicine / feel better
2. cotton / Cotton
3. fever / fever
4. hike / jungle
5. walking stick
6. stuffed nose
7. campfire / looked for
8. stomachache
9. helpful / helpful things
10. hurt
11. in many ways
12. come from
13. made of
14. healed / wound
15. Ginger / root
16. lunchtime / hungry
17. climbed
18. walked / all day long
19. anymore
20. sleepy next to

C Lesson 1

How Do Plants Help You?

Plants help you in many ways. How do plants help you?
You eat food every day. Plants give you food to eat. Watermelon, potatoes, and carrots come from plants. You wear clothes. Look at your clothes. Are they made of cotton? Some clothes are made of cotton. Cotton comes from a plant. Paper, tissue, and toys are made of wood. Wood comes from trees.
Some plants are used as medicine. When you are sick, some plants can make you feel better. If you have a stuffed nose, try some mint. It helps clear your nose.
Aloe vera is a very helpful plant. It is green and juicy. People make helpful things with aloe vera. If you hurt your skin, put some aloe gel on it. It helps heal your skin. If your skin is dry, put some aloe cream on it. Your skin will not feel dry. If you are dirty, wash with aloe soap. Aloe soap helps clean your skin.
Ginger is another helpful plant. Ginger is a root. If you have a stomachache, drink some ginger in tea or juice. It helps settle your stomach. If you have a fever, eat or drink some ginger. It helps cool your fever. Ginger can also be used in food or candy.
Plants are helpful in your life. They give you food, clothes, medicine, and many other things.

D Lesson 2

A Girl Named Jungle Jen

Please meet the girl, Jungle Jen. Do you know why her name is Jungle Jen? She likes to hike in the jungle.
One day, Jungle Jen was hiking in the jungle. She saw a big rock. Jen climbed the big rock. But she fell down. She hurt her hand. She needed some medicine to put on her hand.
Jen looked for an aloe vera plant. When she found one, she put aloe gel on her hand. Soon, her hand did not hurt anymore.
Jen was happy because the plant healed her wound.
It was lunchtime. Jungle Jen felt hungry, so she found a mango tree. Jen loves to eat mangoes. Soon, she was not hungry anymore.
After eating, Jungle Jen walked in the jungle all day long. She felt tired. She looked for a stick. Jen found a good walking stick. She didn't feel tired anymore. That evening, Jungle Jen began to get cold. She wanted to make a campfire. She looked for some wood. When she found some, Jen made a campfire. She was warm and felt sleepy next to the campfire. She wanted to sleep. She looked for some big leaves. When she found some, she made a soft bed. That night, Jungle Jen slept very well. She was happy to have many helpful plants in the jungle.

UNIT 5 — Unique Food from around the World
p.20

A
1. insect
2. bug
3. fried food
4. a mound of rice
5. snack
6. decorate
7. flavor
8. ingredient
9. dip
10. crunchy
11. 독특한
12. 설명하다
13. 인기 있는, 대중적인
14. …만큼 ~한
15. 메뚜기
16. 특별한
17. 바퀴벌레
18. 단백질
19. ~에 흥미가 있다
20. 딱정벌레

B
1. researched / insects
2. bugs
3. fried food
4. oil / mound of rice
5. sweet snack
6. Last / decorated
7. garlic / flavor
8. ingredients
9. dipped
10. crunchy / taste
11. unique / around the world
12. explain
13. popular dish / fried
14. as big as
15. grasshoppers / as
16. many kinds of / special
17. carefully / cockroaches / scorpions
18. raise / protein
19. were / interested
20. Under / beetles / worms

C

What Unique Food!

Name: Charlie   Date: May 7
Instructions: Write about some of the unique dishes that people eat around the world. Then, explain how they are cooked.

I researched some unique dishes made with insects around the world. They are as follows:

1. Name of the Food: Deep Fried Tarantula
   Country: Cambodia

In Cambodia, a popular dish is deep fried tarantula. Tarantulas are large spiders. They are as big as an adult's palm. This food is a sweet snack that kids like. The spiders are fried in oil and sometimes are covered with sugar. At other times, they are dipped in salt. They taste like chicken and potato chips.

2. Name of the Food: Crunchy Grasshopper
   Country: Thailand

In Thailand, people like eating crunchy grasshoppers. The grasshoppers are as long as a finger. First, they fry the grasshoppers in oil. Then, garlic and herbs are added for flavor. They are crunchy and taste good.

3. Name of the Food: Insect Sushi
   Country: Japan

In Japan, some people use many kinds of insects to make a special sushi. They carefully select insects like cockroaches, bees, and scorpions. The insects are fried in oil, and then they are put on a mound of rice. The crunchy fried insects with the sweet and sour rice make a wonderful taste.

People think insects are healthy and tasty. In fact, insects are full of protein. These days, we have to raise lots of cows and pigs to get protein. But we don't need to raise insects. They can be a perfect food source. How about trying some insects as a special food?

D

Lunch with Mariko

Mariko was the nicest woman in our village. She always had a smile on her face. One day, she invited my friend Thomas and me to lunch. We were excited. We wondered what she would cook. We arrived for lunch at noon. "Welcome, boys. Lunch is almost ready," she said. From the kitchen, we smelled fried food. It smelled great. We watched Mariko cook. First, Mariko fried some things in oil. They were fat and brown. Next, she fried some large and black things. She put them on a mound of rice. They looked like sushi. Last, she decorated them with yellow and pink flowers and green leaves.

"Okay, boys. Try these first. If you like them, I'll make more," said Mariko.

We were both interested in trying them. I said, "Okay, Thomas. You eat the black one, and I'll eat the brown one. Are you ready? On the count of three: one, two, three."

Crunch! Squish! We both ate them. I looked at Thomas. I saw his eyes open wide. A large smile appeared on his face. He liked the sushi. And I liked it, too.

"So, boys, do you like them?" asked Mariko.

"More, please," we said.

"Sure! Let's get some ingredients for more food," said Mariko.

We followed Mariko outside. She walked to some green bushes. She picked up a large rock. Under the rock were beetles, worms, and spiders. Mariko picked up the bugs and insects. Thomas and I were shocked. She had cooked them for lunch. Eww!

6 UNIT — An Amazing Story

p.24

A 1. dolphin   2. plastic
3. aquarium   4. whistle
5. trick   6. amazing
7. swallow   8. smart
9. remove   10. save
11. 소화하다   12. 위, 복부
13. 싸다, 몸을 감싸다
14. 조련사, 훈련시키는 사람, 트레이너
15. 호르륵, 짹짹   16. 지느러미발, 물갈퀴
17. 뒤로 공중돌기(를 하다)   18. 자원봉사자, 지원자
19. 첨벙거리다, 물을 끼얹다   20. 담그다, 흠뻑 적시다

B 1. dolphins   2. plastic
3. dolphins / aquarium   4. whistle
5. whistle / tricks   6. amazing
7. swallowed   8. smart
9. remove / failed   10. called / agreed / save
11. digest   12. stomachs
13. wrapped / teeth   14. trainer
15. Tweet / side   16. wave / flippers
17. backflip
18. dolphins / trick / volunteer
19. straight / jump / Splash
20. soak / look at

C

Lucky Dolphins

Do you want to hear an amazing story?
It all began in the town of Fushun, China. Two dolphins were swimming in an aquarium. There was plastic in the pool, and they swallowed some. But the dolphins couldn't digest the plastic. The plastic hurt their stomachs. Soon, they stopped eating their food. The workers were worried. They tried to remove the plastic from their stomachs. But they failed. The dolphins became very weak. If the plastic could not be removed, the dolphins would die.
One of the workers had an idea. He remembered Bao Xishun, the world's tallest man. He was 2.36 meters tall, and his arms were 1.06 meters long. The worker thought that Bao could save the dolphins. He could reach inside the dolphins' stomachs with his long arms. Then, he could take out the plastic. The worker called Bao, and he agreed to help save the dolphins. Workers opened the dolphins' mouths. Then, they wrapped towels around the dolphins' teeth. Now the dolphins'

teeth couldn't hurt Bao. With his long arms, Bao reached inside the dolphins' stomachs. He took out the plastic. Bao saved the dolphins.
Today, the dolphins are happy again. Many people come to see them in their aquarium. And it is all thanks to the world's tallest man. What an amazing story!

D

Those Amazing Dolphins!

Hello, everyone. My name is Dave. I am a dolphin trainer at this aquarium. My dolphins are very smart. I trained them with my whistle. When they hear my whistle, they do tricks. Watch. Tweet! The dolphins come to my side. Tweet, tweet! They wave their flippers at you. Everyone, say hello to my lovely dolphins.
I also trained my dolphins to read. I will show them this card. My lovely dolphins, read the words on this card.
• Jump high in the air and do a backflip.
Now, show me the trick. Watch the dolphins swim off like a flash of lightning. Look how they jump high in the air and do a backflip.
Everyone, are you enjoying the show? This time, I will not blow my whistle. Shh! Everybody, this will be my dolphins' best trick.
I need a volunteer. Over there! The boy with a red shirt. What about you? Can you write some tricks on this card? Thank you! Shh~~! This time, I will not show it to the dolphins. Dolphins, show us the tricks that are written on the card. Look! They jump through two hoops. Wait. Where are they going? They're coming straight at me. They jump high in the air... Splash! Oh, my gosh! They soak me with water. Let's look at the card.
• Jump through two hoops. Then, soak Dave with water.
Look! They did the tricks without reading the card. Oh, those amazing dolphins!

A 1. hand gestures 2. slap
3. stadium 4. sword
5. spear 6. positive
7. gladiator 8. audience
9. celebrate 10. communicate
11. 뜻, 의미 12. 엄지손가락
13. ～보다 더 많은, ～ 이상의 14. 군중들을 헤치고 나아가다
15. 군인 16. 경례하다
17. 도착하다 18. 싸움; 싸우다
19. 환호하다 20. 결정하다

B 1. Sometimes / hand gestures
2. slap 3. high five / stadium
4. large golden helmet / sword
5. silver mask / long spear
6. Thumbs up / positive
7. voted / gladiator 8. comes from / audience
9. celebrate
10. Hand gestures / communicate
11. meanings / come from
12. fists / thumbs 13. more than / speak
14. push / way through 15. soldiers
16. saluting 17. arrive
18. fight / fight
19. Suddenly / audience / cheer
20. waiting for / decide

C Lesson 1

Hand Gestures

Sometimes you use hand gestures such as a high five or an okay sign. When do you use them? Why do you use them? What are their meanings, and where do they come from?

Two boys raise their hands and head high. Then they hit their palms together. They might say, "High five." This gesture takes its name from the five fingers on a hand and the raising of hands high. The first high five was done in 1977 at a baseball stadium in America. When a Los Angeles baseball player hit a homerun, another player raised his hand to slap the player's hand in celebration. Now, people use this gesture to celebrate something.

A cute girl shows thumbs up. She closes her fists with her thumbs upward. Thumbs up means "well done" or "good job" and is a positive sign. This gesture comes from the audience in the ancient Roman Coliseum. The audience voted on the life or death of a defeated gladiator. A thumbs up gave life, and a thumbs down gave death.

The scuba diver in the water gives the okay sign by making a circle with two fingers. When you're eating food, it's impolite to talk with your mouth full. In that case, you can use it to mean "great" or "fine."

Hand gestures are a good way to communicate. Hand gestures can mean more than the words you speak. Think of some other gestures that you sometimes use. What do you think they mean? Where do they come from?

D Lesson 2

A Day at the Coliseum

"Hey, Marcus," I shout. "Hurry up. Or we are going to miss the fight."

My best friend Marcus and I are going to the Coliseum. We are going to see the gladiators fight. I don't want to be late. There are so many people that we have to push our way through the crowd. There are even Roman soldiers there. They are saluting each other.

Finally, we arrive. We look down at the gladiators. They are so big. And they look very strong.

"Wow, Antony," says Marcus. "Look at Spartacus over there. He has a large golden helmet on his head. In his hand, he has a sharp sword. I hope he wins."

"No way," I tell Marcus. "I like Maximus. He has a silver mask on his face. In his hand, he has a long spear. I hope he wins."

The fight begins. Both gladiators fight well. The crowd is cheering. They are enjoying the fight. Marcus and I are enjoying the fight, too. Soon, the fight is over. Spartacus, with the golden helmet, fought very well. He won the fight. Now, both gladiators stand in the middle of the Coliseum. They are waiting for the audience to decide if Maximus lives or dies.

Suddenly, everyone in the audience begins to cheer. Marcus and I cheer, too. Then, we all give the thumbs-up gesture. Maximus fought well. We want him to live.

Walking home, Marcus and I are happy. What a great day at the Coliseum!

Spartacus and Maximus are both great gladiators. I wonder who will win the next time.

A 1. stitch
2. uniform
3. bump
4. fuzz
5. pitcher
6. direction
7. surface
8. bounce
9. teammate
10. grip
11. 잃다, 분실하다
12. (공 등을) 받다, 잡다
13. 공간, 여백
14. 던지다
15. 분실물 취급소
16. 선반
17. 공중에
18. ~쪽으로
19. (공 등을) 차다
20. 득점, 점수

B 1. throw / feel / stitches
2. First / puts on / uniform
3. bumps
4. fuzz / bounce
5. Pitchers / throw
6. baseball / direction
7. fuzzy surface
8. bounce / spin
9. teammate
10. bumps / grip
11. lost / Have / seen
12. goalkeeper / catch
13. answer / spaces
14. throw / into the net
15. leave / lost and found
16. on top of / shelf
17. in the air
18. toward
19. kicks
20. score

C

Missing Balls

Hi, everyone.
I lost my bag with four balls. Have you seen my balls? If you have seen them, please give them to me. They are my balls.
My basketball is big and orange. When you hold it, it feels bumpy. My baseball is small, hard, and white. When you throw it, you can feel the stitches on it. My tennis ball is small, soft, and yellow. When you hold it, it feels fuzzy. Last, my soccer ball is big and round. When you kick my soccer ball, it feels hard. I love my balls a lot. Please find my balls.
Thank you,

From Steven

Hi, Steven.
I found your bag on the playground. But I am wondering about your balls. Can you answer my questions in the spaces below?
Question 1: Your basketball has small bumps on its surface. Why?

→ The small bumps help you grip the ball well. Basketball players grip it in their hand and throw it into the net.
Question 2: Your baseball has red stitches on it. Why?
→ The stitches in a baseball help it curve and change direction in the air. Pitchers can throw the baseball wherever they want.
Question 3: Your tennis ball has a fuzzy surface. Why?
→ The fuzz on a tennis ball helps the ball bounce on a racket. Tennis players can bounce and spin the ball well with a racket.
If you write your answers in the spaces correctly, I will leave your balls at the lost and found.
From Russell

D

Game Day

Scott plays on a soccer team. He is getting ready for a game today. First, Scott puts on his blue uniform. Then, he puts on his soccer shoes. Next, he gets his bag. Last, he gets his soccer ball. Oh no! He cannot find his soccer ball.
Scott looks on top of the shelf. His ball is not there. Scott looks behind the door, next to the locker, and under the bench. It is not in those places either. Scott is feeling worried. Where could it be? Suddenly, Scott has an idea. He looks inside his bag. Aha! There is his ball. Now, he can go to the game.
The soccer game starts with the whistle. "Hey, over here," calls Scott. He wants the ball. His teammate passes him the ball. The ball is high in the air. Scott uses his head to bounce the ball into the net. It is a goal!
"Yay," yells Scott.
The score is 1-0. They can win the game.
Scott has the ball. He runs toward the net.
"Kick! Kick!" yell Scott's teammates. But he does not kick the ball to the net because the goalkeeper is ready to catch the ball. Scott passes the ball to a teammate. Now, the goalkeeper cannot catch the ball. Scott's teammate kicks the ball into the net. Now, the score is 2-0.
"Hooray, we won," yells Scott.
The game is over. Scott and his teammates are happy to win the game.
Today is a wonderful day.

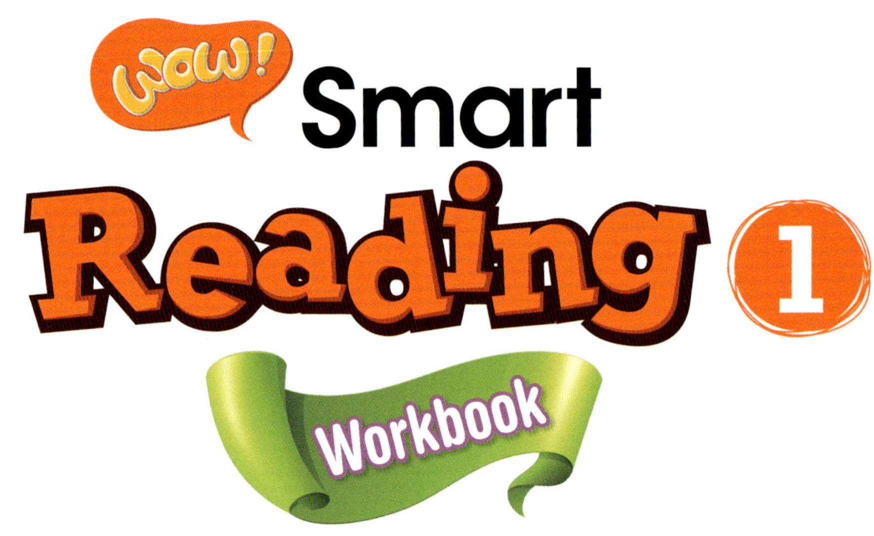

WOW! Smart Reading 1 Workbook